THREE LECTURES
ON COMMERCE AND ONE ON
ABSENTEEISM

LSE Scarce Tracts in Economics

II

THE LONDON SCHOOL OF ECONOMICS
SCARCE TRACTS IN ECONOMICS SERIES

THREE LECTURES
ON COMMERCE AND ONE ON
ABSENTEEISM

Mountifort Longfield

ROUTLEDGE/THOEMMES PRESS

Published in 1996 by

Routledge/Thoemmes Press
11 New Fetter Lane
London EC4P 4EE

in association with
The London School of Economics

This is a reprint of the first edition of 1835

Printed and bound in Great Britain by
Antony Rowe Ltd., Chippenham, Wiltshire

Routledge/Thoemmes Press is a joint imprint
of Routledge and Thoemmes Antiquarian Books Ltd.

British Library Cataloguing-in-Publication Data
A CIP record of this work is available from the British Library

Three Lectures on Commerce and one on Absenteeism
ISBN 0-415-14386-1

Publisher's Note
The publisher has gone to great lengths to ensure the
quality of this reprint but points out that
some imperfections in the original may be apparent.

THREE LECTURES

ON COMMERCE,

AND ONE

ON ABSENTEEISM,

DELIVERED IN MICHAELMAS TERM, 1834,

BEFORE THE UNIVERSITY OF DUBLIN.

BY MOUNTIFORT LONGFIELD, LL. D.

ARCHBISHOP WHATELY'S PROFESSOR OF POLITICAL ECONOMY.

DUBLIN.

MILLIKEN AND SON, GRAFTON STREET.

BOOKSELLERS TO THE UNIVERSITY.

B. FELLOWES, LUDGATE STREET, LONDON.

1835.

LECTURE I.

GENTLEMEN,—It is scarcely possible to estimate too highly the advantages which nations derive from a commercial intercourse with each other. By it each man may be said to possess every power natural or acquired, which is possessed by any of the human race. He can exchange the works of his own peculiar faculties, against the products of those possessed by his fellow men ; and thus in turn partake of the advantages of every variety of power or knowledge which has been bestowed upon mankind. The free intercourse to which commerce leads, has also been the principal means by which the blessings of civilization, and religion, and knowledge have been diffused throughout the world; and thus the spark that is kindled in one country, quickly spreads into a flame which illuminates every other nation.

By commerce too, the advantages of every soil

B

and climate are imparted to all the globe, and the
disadvantages by which they are frequently attended
in their native place, do not accompany them to the
foreign countries which participate in the enjoyments.   Thus we enjoy the spicy products of
the torrid zone, without being scorched by the
heat of the tropic sun, which was necessary to call
them into existence, and to nourish them to matu-
rity.   We have every gift which the arctic regions
yield, without shivering under the inclemency of
a polar sky.   And countless tracts of uncultivated
forests are ready to supply us with ample stores
of timber, without oppressing us by their gloomy
shade.   We need not all be pent in populous cities,
yet we may all possess the advantages which they
afford ; and enjoying all the blessings which an old
and densely peopled country can bestow upon its
inhabitants, we may at the same time have an abundance of those articles which thinly peopled regions
can alone supply.   In short, commerce has enabled
us to unite all those enjoyments which nature has
apparently declared to be inconsistent.   Neither
are the enjoyments of any nation diminished by
thus imparting them freely to the rest.   On the
contrary, each receives in exchange something
which in its estimation is more valuable than what
it parts with.

A feeble sophism is involved in the argument,
that as all commerce consists merely of an exchange

of equivalents, it never can be productive of increased wealth to any people. What is in the term wealth? What can it aim at more than to procure us all we can want or wish, unless we descend to consult the imbecile and depraved taste of the miser, who loves to look on heaps of useless ore? As to the things exchanged being always of equal value, it is the power of being exchanged by commerce that increases the value of each and renders them equivalent : in every exchange a person receives an article of equal value, and of greater utility to him, than that with which he parts, and in many cases he parts with that which to him would be of no use at all.

Since then the advantages to be derived from free unrestrained commerce are so numerous and important, we ought not hastily to reject its blessings or restrict its course. And yet a mistaken view, and a consequently exaggerated opinion, of the goods to be derived from it, has led nations, sometimes injuriously to diminish them, and not unfrequently to reject them altogether. Hence there is no occasion on which so many appeals have been made to non-existing experience as in support of those theories respecting trade and commerce, which are most adverse to the principles of Political Economy. Certain principles have been promulgated (in general by individuals interested in their support), and although they have never been completely enforced, and although the attempt to bring them into operation has never been attended by any useful result, yet all arguments to prove their absurdity are invariably met by a reference to experience, and this is done, although as far as experience can be referred to in this dispute, it is found to be on the side of what is contemptuously called mere theory.

Indeed this is one of the many cases in which, without careful reasoning, it is difficult or even impossible to understand the lessons of experience. So numerous are the effects which follow from every institution, so different are they from each other in kind and degree, and so similar are they in many cases to the effects which other causes might produce, that without the aid of careful reasoning it would not be possible to discuss and collect all the consequences arising from any change in our commercial institutions, and to strike the balance of the good and evil results. In this therefore, as in other cases, the more room there is for doubt, the more we find men disposed to dogmatize.

From very early ages legislation has interfered, and still interferes to regulate trade and commerce. One of the earliest instances of which we find any account in history, was the Athenian law prohibiting the exportation of figs of a certain excellent quality. Assuming for a moment, (though on very slight authority,) that there was in fact such a law, the legislators probably reasoned thus—that the people derived much pleasure from eating those figs, and that the more were exported the fewer would remain for home consumption. But they did not appear to have reflected that, by prohibiting the exportation, they discouraged the cultivation of those figs. They thus in part counteracted the object which they had directly in view, and at the same time they did an injury of which they were unable to estimate the magnitude, by depriving many of the means of exerting their industry with profit in the cultivation of figs for exportation, and thus depriving the public of the returns that would have been received in exchange for those exports.

This early instance of injudicious legislation, however, had in view the natural end of commerce. The object of the prohibition was to have within the country as large a quantity as possible of the commodities which the people desired to enjoy. Modern legislation upon this point has been more complex in the means which it has adopted, and more varied in regard to the ends which it has had in view. Let me here make a few observations to explain the motives and arguments which have led to the doctrines which, in the middle of the last century, seem to have obtained almost universal acquiescence.

It may be remarked that few people entertain very earnest desires for things which they do not perceive to be enjoyed by others, or which they never have themselves enjoyed. Thus, in ruder ages, the wealthy were supposed to be in the possession of every comfort and every luxury, although they had not it in their power to procure many things which are now almost reckoned among the first necessaries of life. They did not feel the want of things of which they did not suspect the existence. You probably have all frequently met with the observation, that Augustus Cæsar, the emperor of the world, had not a chimney to his house, a pane of glass to his windows, nor a shirt on his back. Thus, as we have never felt, we cannot appreciate the advantages which a more extended commerce might confer upon the world. And now many people are disposed to value commerce merely because they suppose it gives the people the means of earning those comforts which are produced within the country; and which in fact, if there were no foreign commerce, might be produced in as much abundance, and distributed as usefully as they are at present.

In the present times a rude observer might imagine that there was abundance of every necessary comfort and luxury for sale. He would plainly see that the only circumstance that deprived him of any thing he wished for, was the want of money to purchase it. Give him money enough, and he can easily procure every thing he desired. Does it not

appear a natural inference to say, if we all had
money enough, we could all buy every thing we
wanted.   Hence the anxiety that has existed for the
discovery of the philosopher's stone, as an instru-
ment of good to mankind.   Hence also, the scarcely
less absurd endeavour to benefit the country by
producing what was called a favourable, that is in
reality, an unfavourable balance of trade.   It was
imagined, that if we exported more goods than we
imported, we should receive the difference in money,
and thus increase our power of purchasing the conveniences of life.

Another class of persons, who would naturally
imagine that a country would derive great advantage from the possession of large stores of money,
consists of those who wish to dispose of their goods
or their labour.   These people see that there are
numbers who desire to possess the goods which they
themselves are anxious to part with.   Nothing
except money appears to be wanting to gratify the
wishes of both parties.   In the same manner the
debtor and the creditor, he who cannot pay his debts,
and he who is unable to procure payment of those
which are due to him, all alike lament the scarcity
of money among themselves or their neighbours.

As money is used as the general medium of
exchange, it is also naturally resorted to as the
measure of value.   I have observed that the rea-
diest way to give a precise notion of a man's wealth

is to say how much money he is worth : and as the more money he is said to have, the richer he is, so it was supposed that the more money is in a country, the richer it must be. All these circumstances concur to create and foster the delusion that considers wealth and money as synonimous.

When people discourse about trade, this delusion acquires increased force. As the object of an individual who engages in any trade, is to increase his wealth or to make money, and provided he attains this object, he is indifferent to the nature of the articles in which he deals; so the proper object of a nation's commerce was supposed to be to gain money, that is, gold and silver, the materials out of which money is made. We find this doctrine inculcated by Locke, and by almost all the persons of that period, who were distinguished for commercial or political wisdom. Locke was in some degree influenced in his opinions upon this head, by a consideration of the durability of money, which is not consumed like other commodities, but merely transferred from one person to another.

To effect the object, supposed to be so desirable, of increasing the quantity of the precious metals in the kingdom, the obvious and simple plan was first adopted of prohibiting the exportation, and encouraging the importation of the precious metals. The restraint that this imposed upon our commerce, especially upon that which we maintained with

India, led to its abolition, and a more complex system was introduced in its place. This was called the mercantile system, and it is not without its partisans, even in the present day.

By the mercantile system, the trade of a nation was considered, like that of an individual merely to be a mode of making money. But even this analogy they did not carry on with accuracy. In taking the accounts of an individual, in order to discover what has been the success of his speculations, it is necessary to take into consideration the value of his stock in trade, and of all his wealth, whether consisting of money or of goods. But in taking the national accounts for the same purpose no attention was paid to wealth of any kind except money. It is true that it would be an impracticable task to estimate the wealth of the nation at any period. But although it may not in this case be possible to proceed with our calculations upon correct data, there is no reason, therefore, why we should adopt a principle that is certain to mislead us. What should be thought of the sense of a merchant, who, from the difficulty or impossibility of of every day computing the value of his stock in goods and securities of every kind, should determine to estimate the amount of his losses and gains merely by the quantity of money he should find each day in his purse?

But we shall presently see that in this system

besides the great mistake of attending to nothing but money, the account of the money itself was taken in a manner that could scarcely fail to lead astray. The attention of every statesman and of all who wrote or thought upon public affairs was directed to what was called the balance of trade, that is, to the relative value of the imports and exports. It was presumed that these must balance each other, and therefore that if one exceeded the other in apparent amount, the difference must have been paid or received in gold. That was deemed a losing trade in which we imported more than we exported, since our money must be drained from us to pay the difference. On the contrary, if our exports exceeded our imports, that was said to be a favourable balance at which the nation ought to rejoice exceedingly. The first remark that will probably occur to the minds of those that hear me is, that on this system every loss our merchants should sustain, whether by shipwrecks, captures, or the frauds or failures of their foreign correspondents would be considered as so much gain to the nation, since the losses would occasion a deficiency in our imports, which, according to the system of the balance of trade, would be considered a proof that the nation had acquired increased stores of money by the transaction. This consequence alone ought to have made men cautious in embracing the system which led to it, and yet it obtained very general belief among all men. Our mercantile policy was formed upon this doctrine, and importation was discouraged by high duties, and exportation was frequently encouraged by direct bounties. The language of this system was accommodated to men's prejudices, and it had that happy degree of simplicity and complexity which is favourable to the general diffusion of any doctrine. Any man of moderate abilities might partially understand it, while at the same time it had sufficient complexity to make the minds of most men rest satisfied with comprehending it, without giving themselves the further trouble of carefully investigating all the arguments on which it was founded, or all the consequences to which it led.

In fact, there are three modes of forming an opinion upon any subject. The first is natural reason, which acts like instinct, and though it may frequently refuse to give us any information, it will rarely lead us astray. The second is hasty superficial reasoning. The third is deep and cautious analysis. The second is a dangerous guide, but the first and third generally agree, and if followed, would lead us to the truth. But the first is too simple for the proud, and the third is too deep for the indolent; we therefore frequently embrace the second, which gratifies at once our pride and our ignorance, and we call it common sense. Or we sometimes change our ground, and when defending it against men who have nothing but what is properly called

common sense to guide them, we support their
opinion by (to them) abstruse arguments, but when
required to maintain it against the objections of men
of science, we abandon those arguments, and appeal
to what we term common sense.

The system of the balance of trade was also found
to be a most convenient doctrine for our rulers.
Many reasons concurred to make our exports always
seem greater than our imports.   The imports were
valued according to a very low and inadequate
valuation, and were frequently introduced by smug-
gling; of course in this latter case without being at
all taken into the account.   The exports, on the
other hand, being subject to no duty, were all sent
openly in the face of day, and their full value, or
even something more, was usually declared.   Hence
our governors were always able to give an account
of their good government, and of our commercial
prosperity, as proved by the balance in our favour,
for which of course they took full credit to themselves.   On the other hand, if the nation was to be
excited to war, or to feelings of hostility against any
country, a little legerdemain in the production of
confused documents from the custom-house could
make out that the balance of our trade with that
country was unfavourable.   Our trade with it was
immediately represented to be a loss, it was robbing
us of our money, and compelling us to pay a tribute
to a foreign state.   Statesmen and writers were
naturally not unwilling to acquiesce in doctrines

which enabled them to soothe or exasperate the people as it might suit their purpose.

This delusion, however, could not last for ever. Men soon became accustomed to what was called a favourable balance of trade, and ceased, in consequence, to think so highly of its fancied advantages, which, in prosperity or adversity, (they were informed,) they had constantly enjoyed. Experience also suggested some useful truths. The great accession of the precious metals, derived from our intercourse with America, led to their depreciation ; and the efforts made by Spain and Portugal to prohibit the exportation of gold and silver were observed to be fruitless, and so far as they succeeded in their direct object, were very far from conducing to the prosperity of those countries.

These truths soon became generally known, viz. That all wealth does not consist of gold and silver. That an abundance of the precious metals, like an abundance of anything else, leads to their depreciation. That goods, in consequence, will rise in price, and require a greater quantity of money to circulate them than before. That from this the nation will derive no advantage, but rather a slight inconvenience, in being obliged to use larger coins than before. That the precious metals will preserve their level of value in every country. That if in one country they are less valuable than in another, they will be removed from the former to the latter, in spite of all restraints and prohibitions, which, from the small bulk of the precious metals in proportion to their value, must ever be ineffectual.   And that a scarcity of them in any country will increase their value there, and thus lead to an increased supply, and that therefore no country can ever fail to possess such a quantity of the precious metals as its wants require.   Being once convinced of the impracticability of confining a great quantity of gold and silver in the kingdom, men were more willing to admit that such an object, if attained, would be of no real service.   That money is only of service by being exchanged for other articles.   That there will always be enough for all the purposes of a circulating medium, and what remains will be rendered useless if we are not allowed to export it for something which may contribute to our enjoyments.

The propagation of those truths gave a serious shock to the mercantile system, but did not altogether put an end to it.   People ceased indeed to think the balance of trade of such vital importance, but the false principles of the mercantile system appeared in another form, and were supported by different and more plausible arguments.   To foster domestic industry, and protect it from the competition of strangers, became the pretence on which it was now sustained.   Our imports, although not considered always as an absolute loss, were still thought to be of less consequence than our exports, and foreign trade was considered useful, rather as it provided a market where we could dispose of our manufactures, than as it gave us the means of importing commodities for ourselves.

This pardonable error frequently originated in the desire of increasing the fair rewards of industry, and it probably would not have existed so long with the influence it still maintains, if the advocates of free trade had directed their arguments against the real motives which influenced their adversaries, instead of continuing to expend all their power and time in refuting the exploded errors of the more ancient system of the balance of trade. I shall endeavour to do my part towards removing existing errors, by exposing the fallacies which lie in those arguments which I have observed to possess most weight with those who still are disposed to advocate a restrictive commercial policy. For this purpose, it will be necessary for me to go into some arguments to which I have already alluded in my lecture on absenteeism, and shall call your attention to some maxims which I think are very evident, and which lead to some important, and perhaps unexpected results.

The first proposition is one of those to which I have already alluded, and is certainly not one of slight importance, nor difficult of comprehension or proof, although it is too frequently forgotten ; it is, that our exports must be governed in amount by

our imports, and vice versa, and that the same is true
of every other country. What we import from
foreign countries must, directly or indirectly, be
paid for, either in commodities of our own growth
and manufacture, or by an exportation of money,
or it must be given to us for nothing. We cannot
pay for any considerable portion of them in gold ;
we must therefore pay for them, if at all, in exported
commodities. In exposing the system of the balance
of trade, I alluded briefly to the arguments which
prove that foreign trade can never deprive
the country of any gold or silver which it
has occasion for ; and that, in fact, people will
purchase foreign manufactures with gold only when
there is a surplus of it above their more necessary
wants.

If the country was in any manner deprived of
any considerable portion of its gold, that metal
would immediately rise in value, and all other
commodities would sink in price. The low prices
here would check the importation of foreign goods,
and would increase the exportation of our own
manufactures, since a less price, owing to the increased value of gold, would be sufficient to remu-
nerate the merchant or manufacturer. Thus, gold
being more valuable here than in other parts of the
world, would, as it were, flow in here until it sunk
to the level of the value it bore in other countries.
These operations are not constantly perceptible,

but the force which, if necessary, would lead to them, is always active enough to prevent any nation from having either too much or too little gold in its possession : the same powers which, if the equilibrium was disturbed, would restore the level, do in fact always operate imperceptibly, yet efficaciously, by preventing that disturbance from taking place. Henceforward we shall consider gold as what in reference to commerce it really is, viz. a mere commodity. It is either a native product, extracted from our own mines by the capital and industry of our own countrymen, or it is a foreign product, received in exchange for our own manufactures.

Similar arguments will prove that we cannot export more than we import, since we will not export without receiving something in exchange ; and we cannot continue to receive superfluous stores of the precious metals, and therefore our exports must be regulated by our imports. The same arguments and consequences will, of course, apply to the case of any other country.

I need not occupy your time with any arguments that foreign nations will not send us their goods for nothing ; and it may perhaps be thought equally unnecessary for me, therefore, to demonstrate the consequences that would ensue from so improbable an event. But it can be shown, that even such unexpected generosity from the foreigner would work our trade no prejudice ; and although I shall

thereby anticipate some of the matter of a future
lecture on production and consumption, I shall give
a short sketch of the arguments by which this may
be proved, as the same proof may be useful for other
purposes, and will throw a light upon the general
impolicy of what are called protecting duties.   Indeed, England has herself been guilty of acts similar
to that generosity which we are disposed to consider
impossible; for the giving a bounty upon exportation is not making a present to the foreigner of the
entire article, but it is paying for him part of its
price.   Raise the bounty higher in proportion to
the value of the article, and we, in fact, make a
present of it to foreign nations.   But observe what
the effect of such a proceeding will be.   If the
French should make us a present of their goods to
any amount, it is true that we shall not export any
of our own commodities in place of them ; but then
it leaves untouched that fund out of which all our
domestic industry must eventually be paid.   Perhaps
an example may make this more evident.   Suppose
the people of England expend, every year, eighteen
millions sterling in the purchase of various commodities, of which let twelve millions be employed in
the purchase of home-made goods, and six millions
in the purchase of foreign manufactures.   These
goods will be paid for by the exportation of six millions worth of English goods, and therefore eighteen
millions worth of English goods will be purchased

either at home or abroad. Hence a hasty view of
the question might lead us to suppose, that if goods
to the value of one million sterling were sent to us
as a present, the effect would be, that we should
import only five millions more in the way of trade,
and therefore we should export only five millions
worth instead of six, according to the argument I
have already stated ; and that thus the consequence
of this pernicious gift would be to deprive our countrymen of that employment and remuneration which
one million, spent in the purchase of their manufactures, would afford.

But this is, as I have intimated, a very hasty view
of the matter. The income of the people was supposed to be eighteen millions, but if twelve millions
are spent in the purchase of our own manufactures,
and, in consequence of the present we received, we
spend only five millions on foreign goods ; that
disposes of only seventeen millions : what becomes
of the other million? It must be spent like the
rest, either in directly rewarding domestic industry,
or in the purchase of additional foreign goods, to be
paid for by the exports of our own manufactures.
I must not now pursue this argument through all
the branches to which it leads ; but I am sure that if
you turn the subject carefully over in your own
minds, you will find sufficient reason to assent to
this important proposition, that it must be out of
the income of this country that the remuneration

of our countrymen's industry must be ultimately
derived.

I am not apprehensive that these truths will be
denied, but their consequences are frequently over-
looked. Commercial legislators are unwilling to
admit that they cannot materially assist commerce
by their restrictions, and that, by depriving it of its
liberty, they cannot make it more beneficial to the
state, or direct its course in those channels through
which the good of the people requires it to flow.
In support of their opinions, it is frequently insisted
upon, that some commodities are more desirable
subjects of exportation than others, and that the
same remark is true of articles imported. That it
is to be desired that our exports should consist
principally of manufactured goods, which have previously given profitable employment to our industrious countrymen, and that it is equally to be
wished that our imports should consist of the raw
materials of our manufactures, or of such commodities as we cannot fabricate ourselves, and that they
should not consist of such articles as might interfere
with the products of our own industry.

The merchant, it is said, will buy at the cheapest
market, regardless of the hundreds whom he may
thereby throw out of employment ; and in the
selection of goods to export, he will choose what will
serve himself, and what he can sell at the greatest
profit, rather than what will afford the greatest

quantity of employment to the poor. The good of
the nation therefore, it is said, requires that the
legislature should interpose, and direct his speculations into the channels most advantageous to the
country.

In these propositions there is a shade or degree of
truth which renders it difficult to give a concise and
satisfactory refutation of this the most plausible
modification of the mercantile system. Its advocates, too, sometimes add a few propositions which
are supposed to be peculiarly adapted to the situation of England. The fullest direct refutation of it
must be drawn from an analysis of the phenomena
of production and consumption, and of their relation
to each other, into which I must not enter now.
Such an analysis would show that the modification
of the mercantile system, which I have just stated,
falsely assumes that legislation can regulate that
which is unalterably settled by the laws of nature.
A single remark upon this subject may show that
the exportation of even raw materials will lead to a
consumption of native manufactures. The sum
received for those raw materials affords an income
which may be spent in rewarding domestic industry.
But it will be said, that if they had not been exported, they might have been sold at home. But
then, those who bought them would, to that amount,
have been deprived of the power of paying workmen. Suppose the wealth of a country is twelve

millions annually, viz. ten millions produced by industry, and two millions of raw materials. Every
article is composed of these two in various proportions. Let one million's worth of raw materials be
exported to a foreign country, and the same value of
manufactures be received in its place. The twelve
millions which, if there had been no commerce,
would have been spent thus :—two in the purchase
of raw materials, and ten in the payment of labour,
cannot any longer be spent in the same manner ;
for only one million's worth of raw materials remains
in the country ; eleven millions remain to be spent
in the purchase of labour and manufactures : but as
only one million's worth of foreign articles have
been introduced, there remain ten millions to be
spent in hiring labour, viz. just the same as if no
foreign trade had existed. The same considerations
will apply with equal force, if we exported manufactures, and received the raw materials in exchange.
I have wandered a little from my subject to expose
the assumptions to which I have just referred. A
fuller consideration of the matter will, I trust, leave
no room for doubt ; but I must defer the further
discussion of it until the same hour on Thursday
next.

LECTURE II.

GENTLEMEN,—I concluded my lecture on Tuesday
with a statement of that modification of the mercantile system, which appears to possess the most
numerous adherents in the present day. At the
same time, I made a few brief observations to point
out the imperfect views upon which it was founded.
In many cases the best refutation of error is the
propagation of truth ; but, in the moral sciences,
that is not always sufficient. Our ideas and our
reasonings are not always so clear as to render it
impossible for us to believe at the same time inconsistent propositions. We are not quite certain that
they are absolutely inconsistent, or we believe that
they may be modified in such a manner as to become consistent with each other, and so be both
true ; or we are not sure that we perfectly understand their meaning ; or we do not place such

implicit reliance on either of them as to allow any consequences from them which are opposed to other propositions in which we believe. We are apt to forget that all the necessary consequences of any proposition are and must be as true and certain as the principal proposition itself. On this account it is frequently not enough, in many cases, to teach true doctrines; it is necessary also to refute false systems, and to expose the fallacies of the arguments by which they are supported.

From what I said in a former lecture, it is evident, that if we prohibit importation altogether, we thereby put a stop to exportation; but it is not in general sufficiently understood that every restraint or duty upon our imports operates precisely to the same extent as an obstacle to our exporting trade; and that as far as commerce is concerned, it is just the same thing whether we impose a duty upon all goods imported from abroad, or foreign nations impose a duty upon our commodities. Commerce is merely an exchange of commodities, and the wish each party feels for the exchange must be such as to counteract the sum of the duties imposed in both countries.

To take the simplest case as an example. Let 100 gallons of wine be worth in England 120 yards of cloth, and let the same quantity in France be worth only 100 yards. I suppose the things of different values in different countries; for it is this difference which gives rise to all foreign trade. Now, let us suppose that a duty of 20 per cent. is imposed upon the entrance of French wines into England. Then 120 gallons sent to England will, by the duty, be reduced to 100. This will purchase 120 yards of cloth, which in France will be worth the original 120 gallons of wine. In reality, in order that the trade should exist, the proportion of value which each kind of goods gains by being in a foreign country should be something more than what I have stated, in order to make up for freight and profit. A merchant would not export wine to England in order to get back the sum which he originally paid for the wine. But as this excess, which is required to return the merchant the expenses of freight, insurance, brokerage, &c. to give him a recompense for his skill and capital, will affect the trade equally in every state of it, I leave it out of the question, in order to make the reasoning as simple as possible. With this rate of duty, those only would buy French wine in England who would give the price of six yards of cloth for every five gallons of wine ; and those only would buy English cloth in France who would be willing to give the price of a gallon of wine for every yard of cloth. Now, let the duty be taken off wine in England, and imposed on cloth in France, and 100 gallons of wine sent from France to England will purchase 120 yards of cloth, which, entering

France, will be reduced to 100 yards, which will be of the same value as the 100 gallons of wine. Thus, after this alteration of duties, the English cloth in France, and the French wine in England, will have the same purchasers as before.

The same train of reasoning may be extended to more complicated cases ; and the qualifications which must be made do not in the least impair the general principle, which establishes the conclusion, that our export trade is as much injured by the duties we impose upon goods imported from foreigners, as by any duties of equal amount which they impose upon the introduction of our goods.

This proposition is modified slightly, but the principle expressed by it is not altered, by the fact that many of our manufactures may be, and in fact are frequently paid for by indirect trade, not by direct exchange. Thus we might export our cloth to France, although we took nothing from her in return. She might pay for our cloth by bills of exchange, drawn upon Holland : those bills will be paid for by goods sent from France to Holland, and Holland may receive payment of them in goods to be imported into England. The same consequences would ensue, though with less convenience to all parties, if the transactions I have mentioned were carried on by means of money, instead of bills of exchange. No money will be sent to us from any country in exchange for our

goods, unless at the same time that country is receiving money from some other quarter in exchange
for its goods ; and unless, at the same time, we are
sending abroad an equal amount of money. In relation to our commerce, all the world may be considered as one foreign country. It is not necessary
that the goods we send to Bourdeaux should be
purchased by the same merchant from whom we
import our wine. Nor is it necessary that our
goods which we export to France should be consumed in the same town in which our imports are
manufactured. In the same manner, it is as little
necessary that our import and export trade should
be carried on with the same state. The reasoning
through which I have led you will be satisfied, if
our import and export trade with the whole world
maintain an equality. The balance of exchange
keeps the supply of the precious metals in each place
proportioned to its wants ; and by that the balance
of trade must be regulated, and not by any regulations which government can impose.

If we examine what encouragement commercial
regulations can give to domestic industry, we shall
find that their effect, in civilized society, is to de-
range, not to protect it. And with respect to the
importation of raw materials, or manufactured goods,
unrestricted commerce will pursue the course best
adapted to promote the general interests of the
country. If goods to the amount of ten millions

of pounds value are imported, they must be paid
for by the products of domestic industry ; and it
does not concern the country in what manner that
industry has been employed.   Its real remuneration consists of the goods which have been imported,
or of the goods which those who purchase the imports are willing to give in exchange for them.   In
fact, the less labour that is given for any certain
amount of imported goods, the better for the
country.

The wealth of a nation consists of the products
of its land, labour, and capital—minus its exports, plus its imports.   Those products, and that
wealth, are divided among the several classes of
society, according to certain proportions, which proportions can be very little affected by the course of
trade.   Every labourer is employed either in working for himself, or for some person who pays him.
In the former case, he has nothing to do with
trade ; in the latter case, his employer will be able
to pay him better wages, if he may turn his labour
to any account he pleases.

The source of our partiality to commercial restrictions, and of many other prejudices contrary to the
truest and best-established doctrines of Political-
Economy, is, that we are apt to argue upon the
supposition, that men's desires are limited, and their
wealth infinite, although the fact is, that their wealth
is limited, and that no bounds can be placed to their

desires. There is no difficulty in providing employment for labourers; the difficulty is to procure the means of paying them. Let me take an illustration which may explain the proposition which I wish to establish. The condition of the Irish labourer would not be improved, his wages would not be increased, nor would he find it less difficult to procure employment if the importation of English manufactured goods was prohibited, or made subject to a high protecting duty. Suppose that we import three millions' worth of such goods every year, what would be the effect of prohibiting such importation? The consumers of such goods would be deprived of the enjoyment afforded by their use, and in exchange would possess the revenue, or the source of revenue, in return for which they formerly received them. Their wants would be increased by the amount of those goods which they could no longer procure as formerly ; their power of employing and *paying* labour would be increased by the amount of the goods which they formerly gave in exchange for them ; but the labour employed formerly in fabricating those goods would be left without employment. If a man's income can command the labour of one hundred men, which he exports, and receives in exchange a certain quantity of English goods, the effect of a prohibition would be, that he should employ the labour of one hundred men in fabricating commodities which afford him less gratification.

But he is not, by the restriction, enabled to puchase the labour of 105 men, nor to give those 100 men higher wages than before : he is therefore so much the poorer ; but his countrymen are not provided with more profitable employment than before. It is to be remembered, that a great quantity of the goods imported from England are consumed by the poorer classes of Ireland. These, therefore, would sustain a great part of the injury that would be inflicted by the exclusion of English manufactures, whereas the proof I have just given shews that neither they nor any other individuals would gain anything by such a measure. Notwithstanding this, we find that those who recommend such an exclusive system assume, confidently, that the poor would gain considerably by it in consequence of the increased facility of procuring employment that would ensue, and that the loss, if indeed there were any loss, would fall entirely upon the wealthy, who could sustain it without any inconvenience.

When I discuss the doctrine of consumption and production, I shall endeavour to show, that all modes of unproductive consumption afford equal employment to the labourer ; and that the quantity of that employment is determined by the source from which the income which supports the consumption is derived. But to prove this at present would involve a digression of inconvenient length.

The direct effects of commercial restraints is not

to benefit the producer, but to injure the consumer.
But a double delusion prevails, which prevents the
truth of this proposition from being universally re-
cognized. On the one hand, this injury is not of
trifling amount, but it appears less than it really is.
On the other hand, a system of restrictions has
always a false appearance of serving a class of
persons who are not really in the least degree indebted to it for their prosperity.

The injury done to the consumer by any particular restriction appears to be very slight. He is
frequently a person of wealth, to whom a trifling
loss appears to be of little moment. He frequently
enjoys an income derived from land or money independent of his own industry; and a tax upon him
has something in it congenial to our feelings, if its
effects are beneficial to the industrious classes.
Even where it affects a commodity consumed by the
labourer, the injury does not appear great. The
commodity in question forms a small part of his
total expenditure, and the price added to that commodity forms a small portion of its price. The loss
to the public is divided among so many individuals,
that it appears to be no loss at all, or else it falls
upon the wealthy alone, who can well afford to bear
it. These considerations tend to support each particular restriction. But when a number of such
restrictions occur, and many articles are thereby
raised in price, the loss to the public becomes

immense, and the injury to individuals a very serious grievance. Still each case is naturally considered separately, and the delusion is thus sustained.

This, and indeed every other case in which the interest of the public is sacrificed to that of individuals, may be compared to a list of pensions, sinecures, and useless or overpaid offices. These, in the mass, may impose an intolerable burthen upon the nation; yet, how small is the injury done to the public by any particular pension, and how great is the advantage conferred upon the individual receiving it.

The stimulus given to industry is in proportion to the rewards of success, and these are lessened by every restriction upon the means of procuring the innocent enjoyments of life. We cannot compute what injury may be done by prohibiting the importation of any commodity, unless we could know the amount of industry to which the desire and hope of possesing that commodity might give rise.

As the injury done by such restrictions is apt to appear much less than it is, so the benefit is certain to be over-estimated. Indeed, it is an over-estimate to imagine that it confers *any* benefit. It is not the protecting duty, but the capital and industry of the inhabitants of the empire that provide food and clothing and shelter for them. But this is not the first view of the subject which occurs to the mind. If a silk manufacture, at which 1,000 persons worked, were fostered and kept up in Ireland by protecting or prohibiting duties, those 1000 men would appear to be indebted for the employment which yielded them support, to the duties which created and sustained the silk manufacture. Speak of opening the trade, and you are met with the answer, " If you admit foreign silk, you will consign to starvation 1000 industrious workmen and their families, in order that the consumers of silk may purchase their gawdy apparel at a cheaper price." There is some force in this argument, and it ought not to be lightly treated. Changes in our commercial policy ought always to be cautiously and gradually introduced. But this observation applies with tenfold force against the establishment of improper commercial restrictions. Their introduction is an evil, by deranging trade ; their endurance is a great oppression to the public while they last ; and even their removal is frequently the cause of much individual suffering. In the case to which I have just alluded, the cause of the mischief is the change. By opening the trade, a number of persons are thrown out of employment, who were allured into it by the existence of the restrictions. But the restrictions which induced them to misdirect their exertions did not create either their industry, or the capital which furnished it with employment. Had silk goods been always procured by importation, an increased demand would have existed among foreign nations for our commodities, and our capital and

D

industry would have been more advantageously engaged in supplying articles to meet that demand,
since every circumstance which increases the
amount of our imports, produces a corresponding
increase in our exports. And if the restriction
had never existed, those 1000 men would have
been employed in manufacturing some articles for
exportation, in exchange for which a greater amount
of silks would have been received than they were
able to produce under the restrictive system. Those
who dread the removal of restrictions, sometimes
entertain an opinion contrary to this, and yet apparently a reasonable one ; it is this :—They suppose
it probable that those 1000 men will not be employed
in making goods to be exported in place of silk, but
that the silk will be procured by the exportation of
the commodities on which they spent their wages,
that is, by the exportation of their wages, and thus
the silk will be procured, and they will be thrown
out of employment. Indeed, so far as they spend part
of their wages on foreign goods, there will be no need
of any exports ; it will be only necessary to cease
importing the foreign goods which those workmen
consumed, and in their place to import silk
of an equivalent amount. Thus, if their wages
amounted to £20,000, of which £10,000 was spent
in the purchase of native commodities, and £10,000
in the purchase of foreign manufactures. Let the
protection be removed, or suppose it never to have

existed, and the consequence apprehended is, that £10,000 worth of native goods will be exported to pay for silk, and that goods to the value of £10,000 more will cease to be imported, viz. those goods which those workmen formerly consumed, and an equivalent of silk be received in their place, and thus those unfortunate workmen will be starved, without any derangement taking place in the balance of our imports and our exports.

This is a fair argument, and requires an answer ; and it can, I conceive, receive one perfectly satisfactory. I have stated it as favourably as I could, in order that when you hear both sides of the question fairly stated, you may form your own opinion. I think, then, that it is not probable, nor even possible, that those 1000 workmen will be thrown out of employment by the absence of protecting duties. My opinion on this point is influenced chiefly by the following consideration. The commodities which those labourers consumed, and which ultimately formed their wages, were produced or imported at less expense than the labour of 1000 men ; for there must have been a profit to the capitalist. Suppose that in their production they cost the labour of 900 men ; then it follows that there will be a source of clear profit by paying this produce of 900 men as wages to the 1000, and exporting the goods which they produced instead of exporting immediately the goods produced by the 900, which is what the argument to which I

am replying, supposes will probably be done. In
fact, it ought never be forgotten, that the produce of
a labourer's industry is effectively the fund out of
which all labour must be paid. One thousand
workmen receive as wages the price of a certain
quantity of bread, and beef, and beer, and clothing,
and soforth, not because they can make silks and
tabinets, but because 900 workmen of equal industry and intelligence are sufficient to produce that
quantity of bread, &c; and that 11 per cent is a fair
and usual profit to the capitalist. If by some chance
invention it was found that 1000 men could make
four times the quantity of tabinets which they can
make at present, their wages would not be increased ; they would even be diminished, if at the
same time any increased difficulty opposed the production of those commodities which they wished to
consume. They would be diminished in reality ;
that is, their power of purchasing the necessaries and
comforts of life would be diminished, although their
nominal amount in money might remain unaltered.
It is the productiveness of labour that secures it profitable employment.

Justice and policy, however, require that protecting duties should be cautiously, not suddenly removed. Those engaged in the protected manufacture have been led to embark their property in it,
by their belief in the continuance of existing regulations. Their wealth, which is a component part

of the wealth of the kingdom, consists of their capital and acquired skill. By the destruction of the manufacture, much of their capital and nearly all their skill are made useless. Capital and skill cannot be immediately transferred from one occupation to another. The loom cannot be turned into a plough, nor the experienced weaver into a skilful ploughman. This waste of wealth will be much diminished if commercial restrictions are gradually removed, with full notice to deter men from embarking their skill and capital in a business which they are warned will not last. To the workmen already engaged in it, the state ought to give advice, and even sometimes assistance, to betake themselves and to educate their families to other occupations.

Although these considerations ought to make statesmen act cautiously and gradually in the removal of existing prohibitions, it ought not to induce us to bear with them for ever. Indeed they are never dwelt upon for that purpose. But the advocates of commercial restrictions sometimes appear to put them forward, just to maintain their cause for a few moments, until the admissions which they were compelled to make may be forgotten, and then the round of argument must be commenced again. Those admissions which are now seldom denied by any one who listens to the arguments in their favour, establish these propositions, viz. That the quantity of employment provided for the labouring classes cannot be increased by any restriction upon foreign commerce, and that it never can undergo a diminution in consequence of the freest importation of foreign manufactures. The universal effect of commercial restrictions is to injure the consumer without benefit to the producer. A duty which restricts importation, must necessarily diminish exportation to an equal amount. From this it follows that the imposition of such a duty throws out of employment many of those who were before engaged in manufacturing articles for exportation, and it renders their skill and capital nearly useless. Yet when any question respecting the policy of imposing such a duty is discussed, it frequently happens that much attention is not paid to this consequence, although the apprehension of the same consequence operates with such weight when any one proposes the removal of any existing duty. The cause of this I conceive to be that the reasoning by which the conclusion is attained is much more abstract in the one case than the other, and therefore is much less calculated to make an impression upon the minds of most men. In one case we see before us the persons who will sustain the loss, and we hear their complaints and remonstrances ; in the other case, we cannot calculate upon whom the loss will fall, though we know it must fall somewhere. Remove the excessive duties at present imposed upon the introduction of foreign spirits, and the distillers foresee an end to their business. Impose a duty upon the importation of foreign goods, and an injury is done to an equal amount to some of our manufacturers of exports ; but who can tell whether the cutler, or the spinner, or the potter, will sustain the loss? We cannot tell until this derangement has ceased, and things have accommodated themselves to the new regulations. In the mean time some hundred tradesmen may have been ruined, but we cannot always connect their ruin with the change which led to it. We are all familiar with this disposition of the human mind. Suppose a tract of quay without any parapet, owing to which twenty men fell in and were drowned every year. If you drew one of these out of the water and restored him to animation, you would feel a pleasing and vivid consciousness of the good you had done ; but if you rebuilt a portion of the parapet, so as to reduce the annual number of victims to nineteen, though you would do more good thereby, yet the consciousness of it would give you much less satisfaction. On the other hand, if by carelessness you pushed a man into the water, who was drowned, you would be afflicted with a remorse that would not quickly wear away ; but if by a similar act of carelessness you increased the breach, so that the number of annual sufferers should in future be twenty-one, the impression made on your mind would probably be much lighter. All this is excusable, because it is natural and

unavoidable, where the feelings only are concerned ;
but we ought to be careful not to allow the same
prejudices to mislead us in our conduct and opinions,
where reasoning alone should decide.   I may add,
that the trade which is produced by a restrictive duty,
is seldom equally solid as that which is destroyed by
its imposition.   Unable to exist in a state of freedom, and not being a natural manufacture of the
country, it drags on a feeble and precarious existence, and is liable at any time to perish from a
change of taste among the inhabitants, or from the
growth and increase of some natural manufacture
which supplies their wants at a cheaper rate.   An
article which requires a protecting duty, cannot, it is
evident, be exported with advantage, since nothing
can be exported which is not able in price and
quality to compete with all the world.   Hence its
manufacture is less likely to receive improvements
from the introduction of a new division of labour,
than those which are made for a more extended
market.   It always happens too, that the workmen and masters in such a trade, are more negligent
than those in other trades which are exposed to
free competition.   They have not the example or
emulation of foreign nations to guide or stimulate
them to improvements. They have no hope to reach
the foreign market, and no fear of losing the home
market, which they consider secured to them by law.
If foreigners introduce any improvement, a further

call for protection is made, and at last the trade dies away in spite of every care to foster it. If the article is one of necessity, the restriction soon becomes too burthensome for the nation to endure. If it is one of taste, those who can afford to purchase it soon become weary of things in which they can discover no change or improvement, and the taste which afforded it its only market is turned to commodities which allure it by perpetual improvement and variety. I shall next proceed to show the advantages which, notwithstanding what I have said, may be expected from custom duties judiciously imposed. I shall mention a few cases which are generally admitted to be exceptions to the rule, recommending a freedom of trade, and shall mention some cases in which I think the principles of free trade may possibly be carried too far.

LECTURE III.

GENTLEMEN,—I have endeavoured to show that every duty imposed upon imported commodities operates precisely to the same extent as a duty upon our exports in diminishing the sale of our manufactures in foreign lands ; our commerce is equally restricted by either, although we may perceive a slight difference in the mode of their operation. But in every country I believe it is more usual to impose duties upon imports than upon exports, and there are several reasons for this practice besides the mistaken idea of protecting domestic industry.

In the first place, it is a convenient and a usual mode of raising a revenue. The income raised by customs is paid partly by the inhabitants of the country which exacts them, and partly by those of the country upon whose goods they are imposed. And although this circumstance in theory, has not been generally known, and therefore cannot be supposed to have been the motive for raising a large portion of the revenue by foreign customs, yet in practice this has been felt as an easy and not oppressive mode of raising a revenue, and therefore, it has been generally adopted.

But if a duty was imposed upon any exported articles, foreign nations would refuse to receive them, as they would plainly perceive that by doing so, they would be contributing a share towards the finances of this country. They would even be able to compute how much of the price of each article which they purchased from us, was paid to the government of this country. They do not perceive that they are doing the same thing when they export to us any commodity upon which we impose a duty. And even if they did perceive it ever so clearly, they could not prohibit exportation to us, and enforce such prohibition, so easily and effectually as they can exclude our commodities from their ports. If they allowed exportation to any place, they would find it impossible to provide that goods once imported to any country should never afterwards be sent here. It would be rather an expensive and inconvenient process to send a commissary of customs with each article to watch it until it was consumed. Besides, a duty upon exportation of any article, and still more, a prohibition, would be severely felt, and loudly complained of by the manufacturers of that article. Each class of tradesmen could estimate the injury done to themselves, by such a regulation, affecting the commodity which they manufactured, and they would generally succeed in raising such an outcry as would prevent the adoption of the measure. An injury to any particular class of persons, is frequently resisted with more vehemence and success, than one inflicted upon the whole community.

It may be remarked, however, and it follows, from some observations that I shall presently make, that a duty upon exportation, although appearing to press solely upon some particular trade, is in reality the most equal tax that can be imposed upon the public.

It is another advantage attending the impositions of import duties, that by their means the nation has a considerable power in regulating its consumption, and of directing the course it shall take. By the same means, also, the nation has the power of selecting the class of persons upon whom the tax shall fall, as a tax upon the introduction of any article falls entirely upon the consumers of that article.

It is much more useful to direct the expenditure of individuals than to control, or regulate, their industry. The interest of each person is his best guide to direct him, both what trade he shall pursue, and in what manner he shall conduct it. But the manner in which the inhabitants of any country spend their incomes, is not directed by self-interest, but by their tastes and habits, in the formation of which, different modes of levying the public income may have a most beneficial influence. The happiness of the people, and the growth of their prosperity, may be materially influenced by the habitual direction of their expenditure. This direction may, in part, be caused by the relative prices of commodities, and the relation of the prices may be created, or considerably modified, by the amount of taxes levied upon each.

It may also be observed, that a slight export duty might have the effect of extinguishing a trade altogether, since to sell our goods at all, we must sell them at the same price at which other nations who do not tax their exports are willing to sell theirs of equal quality. If a tax raises the price of our goods beyond that price, it prevents us from selling any. But a similar effect is not produced by an import duty, which may diminish the consumption without putting an end to it altogether. The reason of this difference is, that the cost of production of any manufacture, is not diminished by diminishing the quantity sent to market. The cost of production of each portion will remain the same, or will even be increased, as the total quantity manufactured is diminished. For this reason a tax which adds very little to the cost of production of a commodity, manufactured in this country, may be sufficient to exclude it altogether from the foreign market. The imposition of such a tax, therefore, may extinguish a trade, while it adds nothing to the finances of the country.

To prevent this consequence, the English not only do not impose any duties upon exported goods; but, in many cases in which the goods themselves, or the materials of which they are made, would be subject to a duty of customs, or excise, if retained for home consumption, an allowance equivalent to such charges is made upon their exportation. This allowance, the effect of which is, that the country sells its goods to the foreigner perfectly free of all taxes, except such as he himself thinks proper to impose upon them, is called a drawback; and, sometimes, although not so properly, it is termed a bounty. The difference in the signification of those terms is, that the drawback is merely the giving back, previous to exportation, the duty which the goods have already paid, by which the foreigner gets them untaxed by us; the bounty gives to the exporting merchant something more, which the goods had not previously paid for duty, by which we pay for the foreigner a part of the price of the goods which he consumes.

But the effect of import duties is different; they may diminish a trade without utterly extinguishing it. The price is regulated by the least intense demand, which leads to an actual purchase; and the intensity of demand, as I explained in a former course of lectures, increases with every diminution in the supply. Thus, a duty of ten shillings a bottle upon the importation of wine, would indeed limit its consumption very much; but some people would still be found willing to purchase a little, at the increased prices. The supply would be diminished so as not to exceed the more intense demand. But if we impose a tax upon calicoes, no diminution of supply would take place in other countries, since those nations who did not impose a duty upon their exports, would keep the markets fully supplied.

I shall now proceed to make a few remarks upon some cases, which many who profess to admit the advantages of free trade, think ought to be made exceptions to the general rule. The first is, where any article is necessary to the subsistence of the people, or to the defence of the kingdom. It is contended that it would be unsafe to allow the nation to be dependent for the supply of such articles upon foreign (which might hereafter become hostile) states. On this ground, many nations prohibit or discourage the importation of gunpowder, or other military stores. This also is the chief argument of those who maintain the utility of corn laws, or high duties upon the importation of foreign grain. They contend that no nation can be secure or independent, which does not raise within itself a sufficient supply of food for the support of its inhabitants. In times of war, a powerful enemy, with the command of foreign ports, might reduce us to the greatest straits. In times of scarcity, those nations upon whose exports we habitually rely, might prohibit exportation, and compel us to endure all the horrors of a famine ; or they might impose a heavy duty upon the exportation of their corn, which, notwithstanding the high duty, our urgent necessities would compel us to purchase, and thus we should at once sustain the inconveniences of a dearth, contributed to increase the revenues of a foreign nation, with interests and feelings adverse to ours, and pay back or lose during a season of scarcity and pressure more than we had previously gained by purchasing provisions at ordinary times at a cheaper rate. It is also maintained that the population which manufactures raise up is less moral, less peaceable, less contented, less happy, than those for whom agriculture provides employment ; and therefore by sacrificing the agricultural to the manufacturing interests, we nourish a denser population, and make a doubtful acquisition of wealth at the expense of the safety, the peace, and the happiness of the empire. I shall not now enter fully into this complicated question, which will form the subject of a future lecture. I introduced it, merely to show the grounds upon which corn laws are often defended as an exception to the general rule. They are defended as a slight sacrifice of wealth, to the security and independence of the kingdom. On similar grounds is maintained the necessity of affording a peculiar protection to our commercial shipping interest. The necessity of such protection is not inconsistent with the general policy of free trade. We may encourage men to enter into the merchant service as sailors, although more wealth might be acquired for the nation if they followed some other pursuit; but we make this sacrifice, knowing that it is a sacrifice of wealth, in order that if a war should unhappily arise, we may have a supply of gallant sailors ready to assert their country's supremacy on the ocean. I shall take some future opportunity of making a few remarks upon the unjust and impolitic custom of manning our fleets by impressment, and upon the fallacies contained in the arguments by which it is sometimes defended as necessary.

But it is sometimes argued, that the circumstances of some countries are such as to demand protection for its manufactures, and I wish to show that this argument generally proceeds upon mistaken grounds. The circumstances which are supposed to render a nation dependent upon protecting duties for the existence of its manufactures, are principally these three : First, high wages of labourers. It is said, that a country, in which the ordinary wages of a workman are two shillings a-day, cannot manufacture goods as cheaply as a nation in which six-pence a-day is the customary remuneration of a workman. Hence it

E

is said, that the goods manufactured by the high priced labour of the former nation require protection against the goods produced by the cheap labour of the latter. The second case, in which the necessity of protecting duties is supposed to exist, is when one country is far superior to another in the skill and productive industry of its workmen. It is said, the competition with the workmen of the former country will either deprive those of the latter of all employment, or will cause a great reduction in their wages. The third is, where the pressure of taxation in any country disables it from competing with the industry of more lightly taxed nations. An answer to those three cases may be found in the manner in which commerce acts upon the wages of labour in different countries, and in which the wages of labour affect commerce.

I have already shewn, and shall henceforth assume, that the relative wages of labourers of different kinds are determined by the different circumstances which make it more difficult to procure a labourer of one kind than another ; and that the wages of any particular labourer measured in the commodity which he produces, is determined by the productiveness of his labour, and by the rate of profits. But the relative wages of labourers, in different climates and countries, is regulated by a different principle. The relation between wages in different employments here is caused by the power each individual has, of changing,

or choosing, his employment.   But, as between the
inhabitants of different countries, no such liberty
exists—as the Polish serf cannot become an English
peasant, in order to raise his wages, so to ascertain
the circumstances which determine the relative
wages of labourers in different countries, we must
discover some medium of comparison between them.

This medium of comparison is easily found in the
case in which both are engaged in the fabrication of
the same article of foreign commerce.   If one man
in England can weave as much calico as two men in
Poland, who employ the same capital; and if the
rate of profits is the same in both countries, the
English weaver will naturally receive for his wages
the same amount of gold or silver, or any foreign
commodity, as will be given to the two Polish
weavers.   His wages will be double theirs.   If the
rate of profits in England is lower than in Poland,
the proportion will be still higher.

To avoid circumlocution, I shall henceforth, by
the expression " productiveness of labour," signify
the amount produced by the labourer after deduct-
ing profit and rent, and every sum which the labourer has to pay for the assistance of machinery,
and for the raw material which he wrought.   In this
sense the relative wages of labourers of the same
kind, in different countries, depend upon the relative
productiveness of their labour, and the relative
wages of labourers of different kinds, in the same

country, depend upon the circumstances which increase or diminish the competition among them.
The degrees of productiveness of labourers of different kinds are heterogeneous quantities, and no proportion can exist between them ; and, to ascertain
the relative wages of labourers, we must find some
medium of comparison between them, unless either
labourer has it in his power to embrace the condi-
dition of the other, or unless the purchaser of the
products of their labour can procure the same commodity to whichever of the two he should wish to
apply.

Now, it is important to observe, that those two
propositions which I have just stated, respecting the
relative wages of labour, may lead to different inconsistent results. Thus, suppose that the relative
wages of a weaver and spinner are the same in
England, and suppose them also to be the same in
France. Suppose also that the labour of the English
spinner is twice as productive as that of the French
spinner, and that the labour of the French weaver is
twice as productive as that of the English weaver.
The consequences of these suppositions would be :—
The French weaver would earn twice as much as the
English weaver ; that is to say, twice as much as the
English spinner. But the English spinner would
earn twice as much as the French spinner ; that is,
twice as much as the French weaver. Thus each
would be double the other. To express the same

result in numbers :—If the wages of an English spinner be 2s. a-day, those of the English weaver will be 2s. also, as their relative wages are supposed to be the same. But as the French spinner does only half as much as the English spinner, his wages will be only 1s. ; therefore, the wages of the French weaver will be only 1s. : but as his labour is supposed to be twice as productive as that of the English weaver, his wages ought to be double those of the latter, viz., 4s. instead of 1s.

This absurdity is prevented by the course which commerce takes. On the supposition I have mentioned, no Frenchman would spin, no Englishman would weave. A territorial division of labour would take place, to the advantage of both countries. If an Englishman can spin 200 hanks of yarn, while a Frenchman can spin only 100 ; and if a Frenchman can weave 200 yards of cloth, while an Englishman can weave only 100, then three Englishmen, (two weaving and one spinning,) will weave 200 yards of cloth, and spin 200 hanks of yarn, and three Frenchmen, (two spinning and one weaving,) will finish the same quantity of work. The six will therefore make 400 yards of cloth, and 400 hanks of yarn ; but if the three Englishmen spun, and the three Frenchmen wove, they would make 600 yards of cloth and 600 hanks of yarn, and, by exchanges, each country would possess 300, instead of 200. The productiveness of labour would therefore be.

increased by commerce in the proportion of 3 to 2 in the whole, or in the proportion of 2 to 1 in the article which each country imported.

It is the degrees of relative, not of absolute productiveness, that determines the course of commerce. In the examples which I am about to give, I shall speak of French and English as mere abstract beings, without any regard to the actual state of trade between them. · This I shall do to avoid minute fractions and complex qualifications. Such easily-calculated proportions as 2 to 1, and 3 to 2, are seldom found in the course of nature. But you will readily perceive, that the truth of the abstract propositions is quite independent of the particular numbers I assume for the purpose of illustrating them. Thus, suppose labour of every kind, with but one exception, is three times as productive in England as in France ; but let the labour in that one particular kind, suppose glove-making, be only twice as productive. The consequence would be, that gloves would be imported from France into England, although one Englishman could make twice as many gloves as a Frenchman. Two Englishmen, by making hats, will get the produce of six Frenchmen's labour ; these six Frenchmen will make as many gloves as three Englishmen, and therefore the English will be able to purchase gloves from the French in the proportion of 2 to 3 cheaper than if they made them themselves. The manner in which this is brought about is this :—Exchanges are effected by the intervention of money as a standard of value. If the productiveness of English labour is three times that of French labour generally, wages in England will be three times as high as in France. If they are 1s. in France, they will be 3s. in England. The wages of two French glovers would be 2s., and these would make as many gloves as one Englishman, who should be paid 3s. Gloves would be made cheaper in France than in England, the inferiority of skill being more than counterbalanced by the low price of labour. In order to avoid fractions, I said that wages in England would be three times as high as in France, although the proportion would not be quite so high, since by the supposition I have made, Eng-lish labour, on account of the exception of glove-making, would not be *universally* twice as produc-tive in England as in France. Thus, inferiority of skill would not prevent French gloves from being exported, and the high price of English labour would not prevent English manufactures from being ex-ported.

The principle involved in the example I have just given may be thus stated. The proportion which the general rate of wages in one country bears to the general rate of wages in another country, depends upon the proportion which the general productive-ness of labour in the former bears to the general productiveness of labour in the other, and the course.

of trade is quite independent of this proportion.
That kind of labour will succeed in each country
which is more productive in proportion to its price.
If English labour is, on an average, three times as
productive as French labour, those kinds of labour
in England, which are four times as productive as
the corresponding French labour, will be cultivated
in England, to the exclusion of France from the
market of the world; and those kinds of labour
which in England are twice as productive only as
the corresponding kinds in France will, in turn, be
cultivated in France, to the exclusion of England
from the market of the world. Neither high wages,
nor low productiveness of labour, can render commerce disadvantageous to a country, or can place
its industry in need of protection. Commerce will
flow according as the proportion in particular trades
is below or above the average proportion.

The next circumstance which gives a direction to
the stream of commerce, is, that the relative wages
of labour in one country may vary by a different law
from that which is observed in another. In one
country, honesty and skill may be rare and high-
priced qualities, and add much to the relative wages
of the labourer who is required to possess them. In
another country, the general comfortable condition of
the people may render the labourer most unwilling
to encounter severe toil, and a great increase of price
may be necessary to induce him to engage in a

disagreeable or unhealthy occupation. In this latter country, honesty, and that attentive disposition which quickly produces skill, may be the general qualifications of the people. On this supposition, if no disturbing causes exist, manufactures which require honesty and skill, will exist in the latter country ; as the labourers possessing those qualities will sell their labour cheaper in proportion to its productiveness. In these two circumstances all commerce may be said to originate—namely, a difference in the proportion of the productiveness of labour of different kinds, in different countries ; and the different scales by which the relative wages of labour vary in different countries.

The principal causes of the superior productiveness of labour, in any country, are—first, the prevalence of integrity, intelligence, industry, perseverance, and general good conduct, among the labourers. Secondly—Liberty and security, which allow every man to choose the most profitable occupation, and protect his life and property from invasion. Thirdly—Abundance of capital, which enables the labourer, on more easy terms to procure the necessary machinery with which, and materials on which, he may work, and the advances necessary to support him until his work is completed. In this analysis it is more simple to consider the labourer as hiring the capital necessary to employ him, and the advances necessary to support him, and paying the capitalist for the use of his capital out of his finished work, than to consider the capitalist as hiring the labourer. The result is, however, the same; and, if the entire work done by the labourer, with the assistance and advance of a certain amount of capital, is the same in two countries, his wages will be higher in that in which the rate of profits is lower. The tendency of commerce will be to export, from the latter country, such goods as require a large advance of capital, for a long period of time, in their manufacture, and to import all goods in making which, the amount and duration of the advances was less than the average period.

The next cause, which is very similar to the preceding one, is the cheapness of land, in proportion to its fertility and other advantages. The skill and industry of the workmen, and the rate of profits remaining the same, the productiveness of agricultural labour varies as the fertility of the worst soil which is capable of being cultivated with advantage. Partly on this account, and partly on account of the scarcity of capital, and the consequent high rate of profits, in newly planted and thinly peopled countries, the trade between them and old countries will consist of an export of agricultural produce, given in exchange for manufactured articles. The thinness of the population, and the consequent comparative difficulty and ex-

pense of keeping up good roads, and means of com-
munication, and of establishing the most improved
division of labour, in new countries, oppose additional obstacles to their success in manufactures.
Any attempts, by restrictive regulations, to raise up
manufactures prematurely in such countries, will
injure them severely, and deprive them of the
principal advantages of their condition.

But of all the causes which have given rise to
commerce, the most striking is the difference of soil
and climate, and the variety which exists in the
natural productions of different countries. Some
countries produce in abundance, what others could
by no contrivance be forced to yield. This difference is frequently so great, that legislative wisdom,
or legislative folly, does not engage in fruitless
endeavours to counteract its influence. We are
content to import our spices from India, without
making any effort to raise them here. And no
complaints are made of the quantity of labour
thrown out of employment by the importation of
spices. To raise the spices annually consumed in
England, how many labourers should be employed;
how many hothouses should be built; what quantities of coal should be raised to supply them with
the necessary heat; what quantities of glass should
be made to protect them from the influence of this
ungenial climate; what numbers of gardeners
should be employed to tend them! In such a case.

as this the simple truth is admitted, that it is easy
enough to find employment for labourers—the difficulty to be conquered, is to procure the means of
paying them.   The possession of mines, and certain
peculiarities of soil, are advantages of the same
nature, and influence the direction which unrestricted commerce will take ; and the advice of the
poet will not be neglected—

> " Ventos, & varium cœli prædiscere morem
>　　Cura sit, ac patrios cultûsque habitûsque locorum,
>　　Et quid quæque ferat regio, & quid quæque recuset.
>　　Hìc segetes, illìc veniunt feliciùs uvæ :
>　　Arborei fœtus alibi atque injussa virescunt
>　　Gramina. nónne vides, croceos ut Tmolus odores,
>　　India mittit ebur, molles sua thura Sabæi?
>　　At Chalybes nudi ferrum, virosáque Pontus
>　　Castorea, Eliadum palmas Epirus equarum ?
>　　Continuò has leges, æternáque fœdera certis
>　　Imposuit natura locis."

To shew that no country can be injured by its
trade with another, I shall make some remarks upon
a few of those cases, in which this trade is most
frequently imagined to be injurious.   Suppose the
case of a rich and highly civilized country, such as
England is, where capital is abundant, and labour
productive, and wages in consequence, very high ;
and of a commercial intercourse subsisting between
it and a poor, and imperfectly educated country,

such as Ireland, where capital is scarce, and labour unproductive, and wages consequently low. It may be proved, that neither can exclude the other from the advantages of commerce, nor interfere with its prosperity. Alarmists may arise in either kingdoms, to say, that the English labourer will be ruined by competition with the low priced labour of the Irish, and that the Irish workman will be thrown out of employment by the superior skill and industry of the English. But there is no reason to apprehend either calamity. The average wages, are regulated by the average productiveness, and one circumstance compensates for the other. Indeed, no one can for a moment suppose, that the stream of commerce can continue to flow entirely in one direction, and that one nation can receive the goods of the other, without giving anything in exchange. If a nation existed, which by its genial climate, the fertility of its soil, and the superior strength and skill of its inhabitants, could produce goods with ten times the facility with which we could obtain them here, we could still maintain a profitable trade with that country, and meet it in the general market of the world. The rate of wages there, would be ten times the rate of wages here. If it were less, their most advantageous imports would be gold and silver, until the abundance of the precious metals there, made the rate of wages rise to the due proportion with the rate of wages here.   Nor let it be said, that we should suffer, since we should give the produce of ten days of our labour for that of one day of theirs: we have no concern with the manner in which a thing is produced by them. The trade is profitable to us, if we prefer the goods we give to those which we receive, and if they can give us an article for less of our labour than it would cost us to manufacture it. The disadvantageous proportion is caused, not by trade but by nature. By dealing solely with nature, that is by producing all our goods ourselves, we should be obliged to pay still more for them. Production is analogous to commerce, it is like a commercial intercourse with nature. Trade is in the same manner analogous to production, it is an indirect manufacture. A ship may be termed a machine for the production of what are called foreign commodities. By bestowing a certain quantity of labour upon some iron ore and coal, &c. we produce a certain number of knives and razors, we may be said to have purchased them from nature. If we export calicoes and receive spices in exchange, the ship has acted as a machine for manufacturing cottons into nutmegs, pepper, and cinnamon.

As every year produces improvements in our manufactures, so every year may be expected to bring some alteration in our commerce. A machine is discontinued, not because it is found to be inefficient, but because another more efficient is discovered; we retire from some particular branch of trade, not because we are beaten out of it by the competition of our rivals, but because we have discovered a more profitable mode of employing our own labour and capital. This leads us to the consideration of some interesting circumstances connected with manufacturing and commercial fluctuations; at present I can only notice them briefly—suppose that England, by the skill of her ship builders and sailors, excelled the rest of the world, so that she could on an average do twice the work of the corresponding labourers in other countries, and that in this manner she has obtained the greater part of the commercial navigation of the globe. Her ship builders and seamen will be better paid, and she will employ more ships and seamen, than the rest of the world. Now, without any change in her advantages in these respects, and without any increase in the skill of the ship builders or sailors of other countries, let England, by her mines and capital and increase of manufacturing skill, acquire such excellence, that the productiveness of her manufacturing industry, will three times exceed that of other nations; one of the first effects would be, in the absence of all restrictions, that her navigation would decline, and that of other nations would increase. Her exceeding superiority in some manufactures would render it unprofitable and imprudent for her merchants to engage in other lines of industry, where her superiority, although great, was not equally striking. Her sailors after the change, should be paid three times as much as those of other nations, and as they could do only twice as much, their work on the whole would not be done so cheap. All enquiries into the causes of the decline of the shipping interest, would therefore be fruitless, if we did not pay attention to the effects which would follow from an increased superiority in other departments of industry. The same effects would follow, if other nations, without undergoing any alterations with respect to their shipping industry were to experience a decline in the productiveness of other kinds of labour. The general falling off in the productiveness of their workmen of every description would lower the wages of their sailors, so that their reduced wages and undiminished skill might give them an advantage in navigation which they did not possess before.

Something not altogether dissimilar to this, is an object of familiar knowledge to us all. The fertile lands of Leinster cannot compete with the hills of Connaught, in the breeding of cattle ; young cattle are never reared in the richest pasture, not that these would be insufficient for that purpose, but because they can be more profitably used in fattening cattle. Much wheat is not cultivated in the vicinity of London, although in the neighbourhood of the best market, with opportunities of procuring abun-

dance of manure.   Every person can tell the reason.   Land in the neighbourhood of London, may
be of value, when used for the growth of wheat; but
its value, when used for building ground, or grazing,
or gardens, is much greater.   Labour, as well as land,
must be paid for according to the productive powers
which it is known to possess, while its value to the
employer depends upon its productive powers, in
the business in which it is engaged.   It never,
therefore, can be profitably employed in any trade,
in which labour of inferior value will be equally
productive.   It is attracted from one employment,
and becomes more valuable by taking another
direction.   These considerations lead me to suppose that there is one case in which it is, at least,
very doubtful whether a nation may not increase
its wealth by something like protecting duties, or
may not, at least by high duties, raise a considerable revenue from foreign countries.   The case to
which I allude, is where a country enjoys almost
a natural monopoly in the production of some particular commodities.   It has often been remarked
that, by a tax upon the exports of tea, the
Chinese might raise a large revenue.   They enjoy a
complete monopoly of that commodity; and, as
they need not dread the competition of other
nations, they may place upon the article the
highest price which it will bear.   As other nations
make it subject to a heavy import duty, it is sup-

F

posed that if the Chinese levied that amount of duty upon its exportation, it would be a clear gain to them, since the rest of the world should then either remit the duty, or forego all the enjoyments derived from the use of tea.

This reasoning is only partially correct. Very little is known respecting the Chinese financial system, and I do not know what amount of revenue they levy upon the exportation of tea. Export duties are, however, more customary with them, than with most other countries, and it is, therefore, probable that among other commodities tea is subjected to its fair proportion of taxation. But it is a mistake to imagine, either that the weight of an export duty upon tea would be borne entirely by foreign countries, or that even if exported tea was subjected to no duty it might not still contribute materially to fill the Chinese exchequer.

Every duty placed upon tea by the Chinese, must add to its price in the countries in which it is consumed. This increase of price must diminish the consumption, and proportionally depress the Chinese trade, and contract the market for Chinese industry. It would diminish the amount of foreign goods, which the Chinese would receive for any given quantity of tea, precisely in the same manner (as I have already proved) as if the duty was levied upon the importation of foreign goods, instead of the exportation of tea. And, for the reasons I have already mentioned, an import duty can be levied with more advantage to the state than a tax upon exports.

This leads me to the second proposition, which is, that the Chinese, from their advantageous position, as the exclusive producers of tea, may subject the goods of every nation to a heavy import duty. Other kingdoms, to purchase tea, will pay such a price as will not only pay the Chinese cultivator the cost of production, but will also pay the tax to which their goods are subjected.

It may even be asserted that every nation which enjoys any great and peculiar advantage in the production of any commodity, may, by its means, levy a heavy contribution from the rest of the world. It may subject the article to any tax not exceeding the advantage which it enjoys over the rest of the world in its production.

Thus, if the English could manufacture hats one shilling a piece cheaper than other countries, a duty of one shilling might be imposed upon the export of each hat, without preventing English-made hats from competing successfully in the foreign market, with those manufactured by other nations. This is true; but it does not thence follow that such a tax may not interfere with the operations of British industry; and, though it is apparently levied from the foreigner, it will ultimately, as to some part of it, be thrown back again upon the British public.

To understand this matter more clearly, we must disengage it from all irrelevant considerations. An unnecessary degree of complexity is added to the question, by the reference to the power which the rival manufacturers of other nations have, of producing the commodity. This distracts our attention from the real—from the only consideration of any importance, and misleads our judgment by a false analogy. A nation is not like a shopkeeper whose trade is principally regulated by the competition of his neighbours. The primary object of the British manufacturer, or merchant, is not to undersell his foreign rivals; it is to sell as much as possible of the commodities, which he manufactures, or in which he deals, and at as high a price as he can procure. His own objects might not be attained, although the foreign merchant and manufacturer were driven from the trade.

To continue the illustration which I have taken from the manufacturing of hats. If we suppose it impossible that a beaver hat could be made out of England, surely it would not thereby follow that an indefinitely great tax could be advantageously laid upon the exportation of British hats. No, although an export duty of £100 per hat would not, upon this supposition, enable the foreign manufacturer to rival us, it would prevent the foreign consumer from purchasing from us, and this would have the same prejudicial effect upon the trade. This example may be thought inapplicable as presenting merely the case of a prohibitory duty. Let us, therefore, suppose a duty of £1 laid upon the exportation of each hat. This increase of price would not probably operate as a prohibition, but it would certainly diminish, and that very considerably, the sale of the commodity subjected to so considerable a tax. We may be certain that any tax laid upon the exportation of British commodities will increase their price, and thus diminish the quantity, which can be advantageously disposed of to foreign countries. That manufacture will, therefore, employ a smaller number of our workmen, the rest must betake themselves to other employments in which the consequent increased supply will reduce the price. As a consequence it will follow that a tax upon the exportation of any commodity, lowers the price of labour in the country which imposes it.

But if a nation enjoyed an immense superiority in the production of two or three articles of very general demand, the wages of her labourers might be, in consequence, so high that she could not compete with the rest of the world in any other manufacture, under a system of free trade. Let us suppose the productiveness of English labour to be ten times as great as that of any other nation, in the production of tin, calico, coals, cutlery, and pottery. The wages of her labourers will, in consequence, be much greater than those in any other nation; suppose them eight times as great, and suppose that English labour is only twice as productive as foreign labour, in the manufacture of other commodities. These latter, therefore, will be fabricated in the rest of the world, at the fourth part of the price which it will cost to make them in England. If a duty of near 300 per cent. is imposed upon their introduction they will meet us on equal terms in the home market, and a large revenue will thus be raised. But if we remit the duty upon any commodity, we shall find the effect to be a fall in the rate of wages here, and a rise in the price of wages abroad; and if this principle of letting in goods duty free, was carried far enough the nation might lose a great part of the advantages which its superior skill in some manufactures, might otherwise secure. The money wages of English labour would fall, and thus her inhabitants would lose part of the advantages which they expected from a reduction of the price of foreign commodities. I have already trespassed so long upon your time, that I cannot now do more than request you to consider carefully the truth of this proposition, which I have endeavoured to impress upon you today, viz. that neither high wages, nor low productive powers, nor high taxa-

tion can ever prevent our industry from competing
with foreign industry either in the home or in the
foreign market.   A nation never gives up one
trade except because it finds another more advantageous.

LECTURE IV.

GENTLEMEN,—It cannot be imagined, that a science so recent in its origin, and so complicated in its subject matter, as Political-Economy is, should at once have arrived at perfection. Still less would it be reasonable to expect, that a knowledge of its justest doctrines should at once be universally diffused among its cultivators, and that no errors should ever exist in the opinions held by any of its votaries. Yet it is not unfrequently made a theme of reproach against the science, that, upon some important points, all its professors are not agreed. And where this disagreement is not itself made the subject of a specific accusation, that error, which, when disagreement exists, must be found to lie somewhere, is put prominently forward, and denounced as the doctrine of Political-Economy upon the point in question. In this manner my subject for this day has raised no

inconsiderable prejudice against the science. I know
nothing which has more tended to revolt the minds
of men, and to cause them to turn with disgust from
Political-Economy as a science composed of quibbles,
and paradoxes, and mischievous absurdities, than the
belief that one of its doctrines is this :—" That absenteeism is not prejudicial to the prosperity of a
country ; that Ireland, for instance, would suffer no
detriment, if all her proprietors should reside in
foreign lands, and would derive no advantage from
their return home to pass their lives, and spend their
incomes, in their own country." Men are unwilling
to study a science which they believe will lead to
results which their understandings and their hearts
alike condemn.

As far as this prejudice is concerned, in order to
remove it, it may be enough to state, that this doctrine is not universally held by all who have made this
science an object of their study ; and that a man may
be a sincere believer in the truth, and the utility of the
science, and acquiesce in most of its generally received
doctrines, and yet believe, as I do, that absenteeism
is most prejudicial to the welfare of a community.

But this is far too important a subject to be thus
summarily dismissed, and I therefore propose to call
your attention to the arguments on which the advocates of the opposite opinion generally rely for its
support, and the fallacies which to me appear to
pervade and invalidate them. I shall also endeavour

to point out the manner in which absenteeism interferes with the prosperity of the country, checks the growth of its wealth, and detracts from the happiness of its inhabitants. I shall also endeavour to prove, that certain other doctrines maintained by the champions of absenteeism are inconsistent with the opinions which they hold upon this point, and that its pernicious consequences may be proved from the very admissions made by those who endeavour to disprove them. The arguments by which the innocence of absenteeism is endeavoured to be maintained are of necessity, from the nature of the cause, principally of a defensive nature ; that is, they consist chiefly of answers to the common objections urged against absenteeism. We must not complain of this ; it is fair and reasonable. Innocence is a negative quality, and those who defend the innocence of anything do enough, if they refute every argument brought to prove its injuriousness.

If absenteeism be injurious, it must be in one or both of these respects. Either the absentee proprietor inflicts a positive injury upon his country by living abroad, and drawing and spending his revenue there, or he injures it in another manner negatively, by depriving his country of those services which he probably would perform if he were to reside at home. I have expressed the latter part of this proposition thus—" which he probably would perform," rather than say, " which he ought to perform, if he were to reside at home; for it is that which determines the benefit of a resident proprietor."

The argument employed to prove, that a person does no positive injury to the country by remaining abroad, and requiring his revenues to be transmitted to him there, usually take something of this form. It is first contended, that if a person chooses to spend his money in the purchase of foreign commodities, in order to purchase those commodities an equivalent amount of the products of domestic industry must be exported in payment. Foreigners will not send us their goods gratuitously. They require to be paid for them either in gold or in other goods of equal value. It is evident that such payments cannot be generally made in gold. So much gold will always remain in the country as will be sufficient to satisfy the demand for it for coin or plate. The payment to the foreigner must therefore be made in the products of domestic industry; and it is a matter of perfect indifference to the country whether the opulent landlord himself consumes his country's manufactures, or sends them abroad in exchange for the foreign goods which he prefers to consume. In either case, the same encouragement is given to domestic industry; as it cannot concern the manufacturer whether the products he creates are consumed at home or exported. But if it is not a matter of any importance whether any opulent person expends his revenues in the purchase of home-made goods or foreign articles, still less can it concern the public whether he consumes them at home, or exports them or consumes them abroad. In short, it is said that a man cannot spend his income abroad until he first spends it at home. If he draws his revenue abroad to spend it there, it must be sent abroad to him in goods made at home for exportation, or in gold or silver or bills, which must ultimately be paid for by the exportation of such goods. The conclusion drawn from this is, that it is a matter of perfect indifference to the prosperity of the country whether a man consumes foreign goods or those produced at home, and whether he consumes them at home or goes abroad to spend his income there.

This argument, like all other arguments in defence of absenteeism, is merely negative. It is brought forward to disprove some particular injury that is supposed to arise from absenteeism; and, to appreciate its weight correctly, we must consider the objections which it professes to refute. Of the mischiefs supposed to arise from absenteeism, one is, that the necessity of exporting gold and silver to pay the rents of the absentees must reduce the quantity of money in the kingdom, or even exhaust it altogether. To this argument I admit that a completely satisfactory answer has been given; and it is only astonishing that such an argument could ever have been supposed to possess any validity. We find it, however, in some of Swift's complaints about the state of Ireland; and he even ventured upon a calculation to discover how soon all the money of Ireland would be thus exhausted. The time predicted by his computation has long since arrived, and wealth, to the amount of several millions, has since been remitted to absentee proprietors, and yet the quantity of gold and silver in the kingdom has increased rather than decreased; and all fears that the country will ever suffer by being deprived of her gold and silver, are now justly derided as unreasonable and absurd. The wealth remitted to absentees, since the time of Swift, has been so great, that it would be absurd in the extreme to suppose, that if such remittances had not taken place, their amount in gold and silver, together with the amount at present remaining in the country, would be found here at the present time. Even if there were no absentees, it would be impossible, by any laws or regulations, to confine such a quantity of precious metals within the kingdom. I am therefore willing to admit that any argument against absenteeism, founded upon the supposition that it is injurious on account of the necessity of exporting money to remit their incomes to the absentees is fallacious; it is founded upon error, and ought to have no weight attached to it.

Another objection to absenteeism is drawn from a similar source, but is put in a more specious form. It admits, that the incomes of absentees are not remitted in gold or silver; but it maintains that absenteeism is injurious, by depriving the country of that wealth which, in some form, must be exported to pay the absentees their rents. It is so much wealth taken away without any return being received in exchange for it. If absentees receive an annual income of two millions, and spend it in Paris, it leaves the country in the same state with respect to wealth, as if the same sum was annually paid as a tribute to the King of the French, and by him distributed, according to his pleasure, among his subjects, or thrown into the sea. When once the goods are sent abroad, and become the property of others, it is no concern of the country how they are consumed. The country is equally impoverished, since they are sent out without any return for them being received.

There is, perhaps, some force in this argument; but I think that the precise point of it is frequently misunderstood, and that in consequence, though it sometimes appears stronger than it really is, it is thereby exposed to an answer to which it would otherwise not be subject.

The answer to which I allude is this:—All unproductive consumption is equally a destruction of property, from which destruction no advantage is derived by the country, except the gratification which the consumption affords to the consumer. If a man, who resides upon his own estate, drinks a bottle of wine, that amount of wealth is thereby de-

stroyed as effectually and completely as if itself or its
value had been sent to Paris, either as a tribute to a
foreign state, or as rent to an absentee proprietor,
or as if the wine itself had been poured into the sea.
In all these cases equally, goods to the value of a
bottle of wine must have been sent out of the
kingdom, for which either the nation has received
no equivalent, or has received a return which has
ceased to exist, and which, during its existence, afforded no advantage to the country, except the gratification one individual felt in drinking a bottle of
wine; a circumstance in which it is evident the
people in general could find neither injury nor
benefit. Every article belongs to an individual, and
the owner is alone concerned in the mode of its
consumption, exportation, or wanton destruction.

Neither is the rent remitted to absentees in the
least analogous to a tribute. In the case of a tribute
paid to a foreign state, the effect is oppressive to the
people, in consequence of the imposition of the taxes
which are necessary to raise the required sum. But
if the amount of that tribute could be raised by a
property tax, imposed upon any particular class of
persons, those who were not subject to that tax
would be then completely relieved from the burthen,
however heavily it might press upon those who actually paid it. Now, the two millions remitted
abroad to absentee proprietors, is composed of the
incomes belonging to those absentees themselves.

If they remained at home, no other individuals would thereby become entitled to it, or possess any of it. If those remittances are therefore analogous to a tribute, that tribute is paid entirely out of the rents of the estates of the absentees, that is, by the absentees themselves : it does not press upon any other member of the community ; and, as it is received by the absentees themselves abroad, no injury is done to any one—no person is made poorer by the transaction.

It is evident that all this leaves untouched the important consideration, whether the absence of the wealthy proprietors may not deprive the industrious workmen of some means of acquiring wealth, or at least subsistence, which would be within their reach, if the former remained at home. This negative proposition is sometimes in part sustained by the argument to which I have already adverted, as used to prove that the same encouragement to industry is given by the absentee and the resident proprietor, by the man who spends his income in the purchase of foreign commodities, and by him who consumes no goods except those produced by his own countrymen. This latter proposition I do not believe to be true. The proofs by which it is supported appear to me to be founded upon a mistaken assumption ; and even if this proposition were true, it would not support the consequence that is drawn from it. It would not prove the innocence of absenteeism. I am sensible of the difficulty of this subject. When a false principle is for a long time admitted, even if one succeeds in disproving it, the consequences that have been drawn still remain, with all their influence, fixed in the minds of men in such a manner, that the arguments of any one who doubts them appear unreasonable or unintelligible.

To remove some of the confusion that attends these inquiries, let me observe, that when the supply of any commodity is increased by any casual circumstances, it is not a necessary nor a usual consequence that all this increase remains undisposed of. Some reduction of price generally takes place, which brings the article within the reach of a new class of customers. The same thing precisely happens, if any event occurs which withdraws from the market a certain number of consumers; a reduction of price raises up new demanders in their place; and by this adaptation to circumstances, the entire supply may still find consumers. Hence it is evident, that the mere fact, that the quantity of goods sold remains the same, is not a proof that the encouragement given to productive industry is unaltered. The same amount of goods may be sold, but at a lower price. Now, something of this sort takes place when men indulge too much in their fancy for foreign commodities. The same amount of domestic industry is employed as heretofore, but does not receive so high a return. The home market is naturally the best, since the producer sells his goods without undergoing the expenses of freight, duty, insurance, brokerage, &c., to which exported goods are subject. If the home market is destroyed or diminished, more goods are forced into the foreign markets by a reduction of price. This reduction will be proportional to the amount of those expenses which I have mentioned as attending exportation, and also to the ratio of the home consumption to the entire consumption in the natural state of things, to the diminution that has taken place in the home market, and to the effect which a slight derangement of the proportion between the supply and the demand has upon the price of the commodities in question. All these circumstances concur to make absenteeism particularly injurious to an agricultural country. It is this, I conceive, rather than the exportation of the necessaries of life, that creates, or at least increases the pernicious influence of absenteeism upon Ireland. I cannot pursue this part of the question further at present, without anticipating the subject of future lectures upon commerce, and the circumstances which determine the relative wages of labour in different countries. It is sufficient for my purpose that you should know how important it is to examine whether exportation takes place in consequence of a diminished demand at home, or an increased demand abroad.

The effects of absenteeism may also be considered in this manner. If a resident proprietor employs a tailor to make his clothes, or a cabinet-maker to make his furniture, and pays them in money, they may spend it in the purchase of commodities to be consumed for their own support or pleasure, and the country, at the end of the year, may not be directly the richer for it. On the other hand, if the same amount of goods as were purchased by those tradesmen were exported to pay the foreign tradesmen employed by the absentee, the consumption of the domestic tradesmen will be diminished to the same extent, and the country will not be the poorer for it. Thus the riches of the country may remain the same, whether its commodities are exported to pay foreign tradesmen, or are consumed at home, but the tradesmen, the people themselves about whom alone any concern is felt, have certainly been the poorer in the meantime. They have spent less—they have had less of those enjoyments which wealth is useful in procuring.

But in thus supposing it probable that the tradesman employed within the year will expend his increase of income in the purchase of such enjoyments, or means of enjoyment, as will expire at the end of that period, I am evidently making a more unfavourable supposition than the fact requires ; for it is highly probable that a considerable part of his increased income will be laid out in procuring for himself and family a better house, furniture, or clothes, and in giving some of them a better education, and in various ways giving them more decent and elevated habits, and contributing to their permanent comfort and respectability. I have mentioned this case, which must be a common one, to show that the country, that is, its inhabitants, may sustain considerable injury by absenteeism, even although the absentee requires that his rent should be remitted to him in commodities, not in money.

This will appear more evident if we consider another argument which is much relied upon by the defenders of absenteeism. They say that industry is set to work and maintained, not by income, but by capital; and that if the capitalist is in the country, it is no matter where the rich consumer resides. The propounders of this argument, appear to entertain very vague and inaccurate notions of the circumstances which determine the rate of wages. But I shall not now enter into the controversies to which this consideration would lead; without doing so, I trust I shall succeed in proving that there is not any weight in the argument. Indeed those who rely upon it, seem to assume that all expenditure consists of the purchase of manufactured goods, and that all productive labour must be employed in some business which requires a long advance and a large outlay of capital. In fact, that there is no money spent, except in the purchase of cotton and hardware, and similar articles; and that all labour is employed in making them. Some such, vague im-

pression, insensibly influences those who use the
argument which I am now discussing.

But let us look at the different forms of expenditure and labour ; and we shall see how little
application that argument has, and how far it is from
being true, that the wages of labour depend solely
upon the amount of capital in the country, compared
with the number of labourers in it. It is certainly
at least not true in the sense in which it must be
taken to sustain the argument, for that requires that
the wages of labour should depend upon the amount
of capital in the country, and upon nothing else ;
and that capital in this proposition should mean,
wealth employed for the purpose of making a profit
thereby, and that it should not extend to any part
of a man's income, however analogous in other respects the latter might be to capital. All these assumptions are necessary to convert the argument
into any proof of the harmlessness of absenteeism,
since it evidently supposes that if the absentee remained at home, no part of his income would be
employed as capital.

Now, is it true that the same quantity of capital
however laid out, will afford the same employment
and wages, to labourers ? Is not the contrary proposition evident ? A capital of £1000, if employed
in a manufacture which returns it in two years, will
give an income of £50 a year to ten labourers,
but if it is employed in a business where the return

is made in a period of six months, it will give the same employment and wages to forty labourers.   Is not this such a difference as should make us cautious how we draw any deductions from the proposition that the employment of labourers depends upon the capital, not the income of the country. The returns to capital are all derived ultimately from income, and the capitalist may be considered as the mere agent of the incomist.

To carry on these observations, I may observe that the change in the employment of capital, which is caused by absenteeism, is precisely of that kind which prevents it from giving that amount of employment to labourers, which it would otherwise afford.   It is admitted, and even relied upon as an argument, on the other side, that the effect of absenteeism (they call it the only effect) is to divert capital from manufactures for home consumption, to manufactures intended for exportation ; that is, from a trade in which the returns are quickly made, to one in which they are received after a longer period.

I fear that I have taken up too much of your time with this discussion of the arguments urged in defence of absenteeism, and I shall therefore only state one more, and make a few very brief remarks upon it. This argument consists merely of the assertion that, even if the residence of wealthy proprietors should raise wages, it must be, by lowering

profits.   This argument is founded upon a most er-
roneous supposition respecting the nature of wages
and profits, and it assumes that their sum is a con-
stant quantity.   It would be out of order to refute
it here.   It is true only upon the assumption that
the productiveness of labour remains unaltered;
but once grant this assumption, and every question
in political economy becomes unimportant.   Wise
commercial and financial regulations, the impartial
administration of justice, the general diffusion of in-
tellectual, moral, and religious education, the making
of roads, bridges, canals, quays, docks, and harbours,
and every institution commonly supposed of the
greatest importance, must all be deemed things of
comparative insignificance, since they can only raise
wages at the expense of profits, or the reverse.   An
argument that will prove everything proves nothing,
and I need not trouble you with any further refutation of it.

I have dwelt, perhaps, too long on arguments
used in defence of absenteeism; but I fear, that if I
discussed the subject in a more natural order, by
declaring merely my own opinion, and the arguments by which I wished to support it, they would
have little weight with those who knew (and is there
any one who does not know?) that the contrary
opinion is held by many men of sense and learning.

This subject has hitherto been discussed by persons
who paid very little attention to the arguments of

their antagonists. Those upon one side have de-
claimed against absenteeism, and relied alike upon
arguments that have been frequently and completely
refuted, and upon those to which no answer has
ever been attempted. Those on the other side with
greater show of fairness, state some of the opposite
arguments, and endeavour to answer them ; but they
do not thus state all the arguments of their adversaries ; and to some of those which they do state, the
answer which they give, is far from being satisfactory.   I have laid those answers before you, and
pointed out what I considered to be defective in
them.

But even if all those answers were valid, for the
purposes for which they are used, still the principal
objections to absenteeism would exist with undiminished force.   These are drawn from the injury
which a society sustains from the absence of its
wealthy members, in a moral and political, as well
as in an economical point of view.   I here consider moral and political effects, only so far as they
produce economic results.   This consideration is
sometimes evaded by saying, that we are only con-
sidering the direct economical results of absenteeism, not those which are indirectly produced
through the medium of moral and political causes.
But this is inconsistent and unreasonable.   The
same course is not pursued in the discussion of
other questions in Political-Economy.   For instance,

are not all the bad effects of a vicious system of poor laws merely of a moral nature? The economic effects, relating to the production, accumulation, consumption, or distribution of wealth, are all produced indirectly through the medium of moral causes. Let us adopt the same principles of discussion when we consider what influence absenteeism is likely to exert on the prosperity of the country. If we stop at the direct economic effects of absenteeism, we cannot come to any practical result, since its indirect effects are infinitely more important, and yet this has been the kind of answer given to committees of the Lords and Commons, when they examined some Political-Economists on the effects of absenteeism, in order to investigate the causes of the misery and poverty of Ireland, of course with a view to devise some means for their redress.

Another mode of evading this consideration, or of rendering it fruitless, is to admit at once that the residence of the wealthy proprietor is likely to be advantageous to the community, if he himself and his family are persons of benevolence and wisdom; but that it will be disadvantageous if the contrary is the case. Those effects, therefore, they say, which vary according to the characters of individuals must be considered as accidental, and not as those essential results which alone are to be considered in any science.

Now, it certainly must be considered both illogical and unphilosophical to stop at a hypothetic proposition, if we have the means of determining the truth or falsehood of the antecedent. And this we can do in the present case, unless we are disposed to doubt that we are social beings. Is it a matter of doubt whether the passions and affections of man, under such restraints as education, religion, and the laws of his country usually impose, will lead him as naturally to injure as to serve his fellow-creatures? This would not be the case even if a man was by nature as well disposed to misanthropy as to benevolence; and even if it was a matter of indifference to him whether he was praised, beloved, respected or censured, detested and despised.

But instead of reasoning too abstractedly on the nature of man in general, let us consider in detail, what the conduct of a resident landlord and his family is likely to be. In the first place, a great part of that income which he spends in ornamenting and improving his house and grounds, and much of that which he lays out in the purchase of clothes and furniture, and all that he pays for personal services of every description, gives exactly the same amount of employment and wages to labourers, as if it were so much capital.

In the next place, farming is so attractive an occupation, and one so natural to man, that there are few resident proprietors who do not pursue it in

some degree. They can afford the risk which attends every new experiment, and the introduction
of improved modes of husbandry, which even when
adopted from the examples of places where they
have been found to succeed, are yet generally
attended at the outset with some loss to the first
introducers, owing perhaps to their ignorance of
some of the details, or to the want of the necessary
skill among the workmen employed to execute
them. Thus although few gentlemen farmers find
farming a source of profit, at least in Ireland, yet
they generally improve the agriculture of the neighbourhood, by introducing an improved breed of
cattle, or better contrived agricultural instruments,
or a better rotation of crops. In almost every part
of Ireland where agriculture is not still in its
wildest, rudest state, you will find that the principal
improvements now in use were introduced by, and
copied from some resident landlord. His education
enables him to learn the practices of other countries, and his wealth enables him to make a trial of
them. It is true that the same thing may sometimes be done by the honest and skilful agent of a
liberal absentee. But this requires a combination of
good qualities on the part of the agent of an absentee,
which ever must be of rare occurrence, and still
there would be wanting the example which enables
the farmers in the neighbourhood, to see the things
done before their eyes, and to copy the parts which

they see succeed, having at the same time the opportunity of employing workmen already instructed in
their business, and of seeing improved instruments
in actual work. How much more efficacious is this
than the most earnest recommendation.

The absentee, if a man of wisdom and benevolence, may do much towards the improvement of
his tenantry, although his benevolence is not excited
by the presence of their distress, nor his wisdom
guided by that knowledge of their actual situation
which nothing but a residence amongst them can
give.

The resident proprietor has every circumstance
disposed to stimulate his benevolence, and direct
his judgment, and even while following his pursuits
merely for his own amusement, he may do a great
and permanent good without having any such object directly in view. The resident proprietor is
more likely to contribute to all works of charity
and public utility, and to promote religion and education in the neighbourhood. He can learn the
exact cause and measure of the distress of each
individual, and by a timely relief at a small expense,
do an incalculable amount of good. He can discover and encourage, and reward merit, which is
beyond the reach of the absentee, who must act
according to some general rule, or commit the
charge to other and less interested persons. In
short, it would be endless to enumerate all the ser-

vices which in different degrees are performed by
the families of the resident proprietors. Nothing
but a residence in the country, and a knowledge of
the ignorances, and habits, and wants of the poor
will enable any man to comprehend fully how great
the good is which a resident proprietor always can
do, and often actually does at a small expense, and
which the absentee could not perform, however
earnest might be his wishes, and immense his wealth.

I may at the same time observe that the conduct
of a good and bad resident landlord, are not exactly
opposite in their effects.   The results are not re-
spectively good and bad, but good and indifferent.
Even if a wicked man were to attempt it, he could
not introduce or bring into general use worse modes
of agriculture. He may manage his farm in the
most barbarous manner, use the most primitive
instruments of husbandry, and feed cattle which no
care could bring into condition, but his example
will find no followers. His neighbours will look on
and laugh. It is only by improvements that he can
bring in any change. Neither do I suppose any
man so depraved as wilfully to encourage drunkenness, neglect, and idleness, and reprehend those
whom he finds to be sober, attentive, and industrious. He will not strive to propagate disease and
poverty, and demolish the institutions of utility
which he finds around him. Thus of resident proprietors it may be said, that one half at least do a

great deal of good, the other half do no mischief.
I have not dwelt upon the political effects of a resident landlord in repressing outrage and crime.
They are all most beneficial in his various capacities,
as citizen, witness, juror, or magistrate.

In Political-Economy, we must not abstract too
much. A fair statement of a question is often the
most important step to a correct answer. We are
not called upon to say what the effects would be of
a person spending a certain sum annually in the
purchase of various commodities of luxury or comfort
among an intelligent, industrious population, who,
as Political-Economy too often assumes, are all guided
in all their conduct by a prudent regard to their own
interests. The question is, whether men with a
certain education and command of wealth, and that
influence which wealth and knowledge confer upon
the possessors, and with that relation to the people
round them in which a landlord stands to his tenantry, are likely, from the constitution of mankind and
society, to do good, and promote the growth of
wealth, and the progress of civilization, by residing
amongst a poor and uneducated and ignorant population, such as we know the people of Ireland in
fact to be.

APPENDIX.

PAGE 3.

On this point, two opposite and false opinions are sometimes entertained. One, that no wealth can be derived to the world from trade, since commerce is merely an exchange of equivalents, and therefore, that if one nation or person gains by trade, it must be at the expense of some other nation or person. That profit can only be gained at the expense of some persons who sustain a corresponding loss: and that nothing can be fairly made by trade, except the expenses of freight, insurance, &c. which is rather a compensation for labour and risk, than profit properly so called.

This opinion is sufficiently refuted, by reference to the personal and territorial division of labour, to which exchanges give rise. In the case mentioned in page 53, by fair and equal exchanges, each country makes a profit of 50 per cent. Each country acquires half as much more of the goods which are the subject of the example, as it would possess, if it confined itself to producing them directly, without the intervention of any exchanges.

The second error is, to suppose, that because of those goods which are exported, a sufficient quantity remains within the kingdom, therefore those which are exported are mere surplusage, from which the nation would derive very little advantage, if they were left at home. Thus in England, if 1000 million yards of cotton are manufactured, of which half are exported, and half consumed at home ; as a sufficient quantity remains for home consumption, notwithstanding the exportation, it may be supposed by some, that the returns received for our exports, are so much clear gain to the country, since they are received in exchange for goods, which, if they were not exported, would be almost valueless from their redundancy. This, however, is founded upon an incorrect view of facts, for the goods which were exported, were manufactured in consequence of the demand for them, which existed in foreign countries, and if that demand ceased to exist, the capital and labour employed in their manufacture would be transferred to some other employment, either to produce goods for the foreign market, or for home consumption ; some inconvenience would be felt in the transition, and it is probable that the goods produced in the new trade or manufacture would not furnish so much gratification to the people, as those formerly received in exchange for the exported cottons : but this latter injury would be much slighter than we should at first suppose it would be.

It should never be forgotten that foreign trade does nothing but supply us with foreign commodities ; and that all those goods which are produced and consumed at home, would probably be produced in as great abundance, and distributed in the same manner as at present, among the different orders of society, if no foreign trade existed.

Commerce is not principally useful as a means of procuring a permanent addition of wealth to the country, but rather as a means of obtaining certain articles of speedy consumption. The trade of a nation with the world, is not so analogous to that of a merchant who conducts a trade for profit, as it is to the exchanges made by an individual, who possesses a revenue not derived from trade, which he expends in the purchase of various commodities, which he desires to consume. The revenue of the nation is derived from the land, and the various works and improvements on it; and from the skill, capital, and industry of its inhabitants. The nation may become richer, either by those sources of wealth, which I have just enumerated, becoming more productive, or by the year's production exceeding the consumption of the year; and those results may take place independently of foreign trade.

Page 7.

Many confused ideas are entertained respecting the power of money, to increase the comforts of the community. It is not difficult to shew that a scarcity of any particular commodity, such as corn, cannot be remedied by an increased supply of money. If the quantity in the country, amounts only to two thirds of the quantity usually consumed in the year, then the quantity consumed must be reduced in the same proportion; and whatever stores of money are introduced, can only have the effect of raising the price of corn, or of altering the distribution; by giving one man more, and another less, than he would otherwise consume.

The abundance of money, can never remedy the scarcity of anything else, except by leading to its importation; and this can only be brought about by the exportation of money. Those, therefore, who restrict or prohibit the exportation of the precious metals—restrict or prohibit the only mode in which the possession of the precious metals can be of use, in procuring for a country, an increased supply of any of the conveniences of life.

But the case I have put is the most simple, and the efficacy of money to produce an increase of the comforts of life, to the community at large, is sometimes maintained by a train of reasoning, which either falsely assumes that money and wealth are the same, or that the quantity of money in the country may be increased by forced importation, and yet, that no depreciation will take place.

The reasoning to which I allude, sometimes proceeds in this manner. If the quantity of money in the kingdom is increased, those who possess it will be enabled to purchase more commodities than before. This will call a greater number of labourers into employment, and these in turn will be enabled to purchase goods, which, while they were unemployed, they could not have afforded. Thus, the effect of the increase of money in the kingdom, will be an increased consumption, and in consequence, an increased production of commodities ; it will give employment to additional labourers, and introduce a general animation and briskness into trade.

The first remark I shall make upon this, is, that it assumes that the quantity of money has been increased, without its undergoing a corresponding depreciation, since it supposes, that by the increased quantity of money, an increased quantity of goods may be purchased.

But if we look farther into the argument, we shall see that it assumes that the wealth of the country has been increased rather than its money. The effects it speaks of would not follow from the increased supply of the precious metals, which a restricted commerce might introduce. It supposes a man in possession of a greater quantity of money than he would have had if commerce had been less restricted, and about to spend this additional portion in the purchase of domestic manufactures. Now, as this restriction upon commerce, cannot have increased his income, as measured in the labour of his own countrymen, (for his income so measured is altogether independent of foreign trade,) his increased quantity of money must have been (and in fact the purpose for which the argument is used assumes that it actually has been) caused by his having been prevented from purchasing foreign commodities to that amount. The result of the argument is, therefore, merely this, that if a man does not employ any part of his income in the purchase of foreign goods, he will be enabled to purchase a greater quantity of lomestic commodities.

This effect will, however, be produced, independently of the importation of gold or silver; and its good is doubtful, since it is merely the substitution of one trade for another, which gives employment to the same number of labourers. The question is usually argued, as if a forced importation of the precious metals could, without depreciation, increase any person's income, or his power of employing and remunerating labour. This is, however, impossible, since this power depends upon the nature of its source, which is independent of foreign trade. For instance, the income of the landed proprietors, or their power of purchasing labour, depends upon the quantity, fertility, and other circumstances of the land; the demand for agricultural produce, and the state of agriculture in the country. His rent, as determined by these circumstances, will be equal to the wages of a certain number of agricultural labourers; and measured in gold and silver, it will rise or fall, according as the wages of such labourers rise or fall. They will continue to preserve the same proportion, notwithstanding any change that may take place in the quantity or value of the precious metals, within the kingdom.

PAGE 43.

When the principal exports of two countries are of totally different kinds, and when each country has an immense superiority over the other, in the commodities which it exports, the relative wages of labour in these countries may vary, in consequence of circumstances which arise in other nations. Thus, if the principal exports of England are her manufactured articles, and of France her wines and brandy, the wages of labour in England and France will depend very much upon the price which the different countries of the world are willing to give for the wines of France, and the manufactures of England. An increased demand for the staple commodity of either country, will have a tendency to raise the wages of labour there. In this respect, a new market, which takes off a considerable quantity of our goods, may be of service to us, although the purchasers there may possess no articles which we desire to consume. It is enough if they can give us any goods in exchange, for which the other nations of the earth will supply us with their commodities. This new market will raise the price of our labour, and make it sell higher all over the world.

Whatever increases the supply of commodities produced by British labour, has a tendency to lower their price, and in consequence, to reduce the wages of British labourers; the contrary effect will follow, from whatever increases the demand.

For this reason, I am inclined to think that Dr. Chalmers has not fully estimated the advantages of particular foreign trades. He rightly observes that the only use of foreign trade, is to procure us foreign articles, and that it does not effect the double purpose of procuring a market for our superfluous labour, and also of procuring us foreign goods. But from this he concludes, (I think on insufficient grounds) that the only use of our commerce with any particular country is to procure for us, the products of that country, that our trade with West India, for instance, is only useful to supply us with sugar.

On the contrary, our trade with any particular country has two distinct possible effects. One to furnish us with the natural products, or the manufactures of that country: another, to increase or diminish the price of our countrymen's industry in all other countries.

Thus suppose a new kingdom discovered, the annual value of whose exports to us should amount to five millions sterling, we should derive from our trade with this country, the gratification which the consumption of their goods afforded, in place of that afforded by goods of equal value, which we formerly consumed.

But the discovery of this new market will have an effect upon the price of our labour, which may be estimated as follows: suppose that they receive from us three millions worth of our goods, and that of the five millions worth of goods we have ceased to consume, three millions had been supplied to us from foreign countries, and two millions worth were the products of domestic industry, then the market for our industry will have been increased by one million. To that amount our desire to export will be diminished, and our demand for the goods of other countries will be reduced by three millions, and as they will have the same desire as before for our commodities, the price of our labour will rise, or that of theirs will fall, until the relative alteration of prices induces us to purchase more of the goods of other countries, or compel them to demand less of ours. Thus the balance of our imports and exports will be restored, but the condition of the labouring classes of this country will have been improved, if the amount of our goods demanded by the new market exceeds that amount, which, in consequence of its discovery we have ceased to consume. This effect may be counteracted or increased by the effect which the trade of other countries with this new market may have upon the wages of labour in those countries.

These considerations tend to show the importance of our export trade, and the benefit we receive from those countries which consume our exports; and may show how, in some instances, judicious restrictions on our trade, may advance the prosperity of this kingdom. This advantage is, however, limited to the easy collection of a revenue, for the benefit derived from restraining our imports will be counteracted by the reduced quantity of our exports which will be demanded, and by the loss of the gratification to be derived from the consumption of those imports which we forbid.

Page 51.

It is a common assertion, and in general a correct one, that taxes upon any commodity fall upon the consumer, not upon the producer. They form part of the cost of production, which the consumer must pay, in order to procure the article. This proposition, however, is often extended to cases, to which it does not apply. A glance at the proof of the proposition, will shew the limits within which it is confined.

The proof is shortly this—If a tax is imposed upon any article, the producers will make a corresponding addition to its price, and will produce no more than can be sold at the increased price; but if necessary, will rather turn their labour and capital to some other business.

Now, this argument supposes, that the labour and capital formerly employed, in producing the article on which the tax is imposed, can be turned, with equal advantage, to some other employment; and the proposition supported by this argument admits of no greater extension. If any disadvantages attend the employment of more labour and capital in other pursuits, a tax equivalent to those disadvantages may be imposed, and will fall entirely on the producer. If it is impossible to change to another pursuit, the tax will, in the same manner, fall upon the producer.

It is undoubtedly true, that the consumer must pay the cost of production of any commodity he desires to consume; and that its cost of production includes as well the taxes to which it is subject, as the profits of the capitalist, the wages of the labourer, in short, the expense of conquering every difficulty which opposes its production. But it is equally true, on the other hand, that the labourer must work for whatever wages he can get; and that goods, to be sold at all, must be sold for such a price as the purchaser is willing to give. The price fixes at, or oscillates about that point, which produces an equality between the effective demand and the supply. From this price must be deducted taxes, profits, and other expenses, and the balance will be the wages of the labourer.

Thus, a spinner in the country will not receive from a country manufacturer the same wages for task-work as one who lives in Manchester. The manufacturer must sell his goods at the same price, without regard to the place where they were made. But the country manufacturer sustains a greater expense in the carriage of his raw materials, and in the disposing of his manufactured goods, and procuring and repairing his machinery. He cannot therefore engage in the business with any prospect of success, unless the cheapness of labour is sufficient to compensate for those expenses. Hence the wages of labourers in the country will be less than in large towns.

But there is a limit to this difference. It can never exceed that amount which will be an equivalent to the labourer in the country, for the inconveniences and expenses of changing his residence to the town in search of employment. Thus, within certain limits, a part of the cost of production may be borne by the labourer in the reduction of his wages, although it appears to form part of the price which is paid by the consumer.

These limits may be disregarded for all practical purposes, when the comparison is made not between the wages of labour in a town and the adjacent country, but between the wages of labour in different kingdoms, such as France and Russia. Here the difference of manners, laws, and languages, will effectually prevent a labourer in one country, from being induced by the hope of higher wages, to remove to the other; and therefore, all the difficulties of producing any article, which is peculiar to one country, must either be borne by the capitalists and labourers of that country, in the form of reduced profits and wages, or the manufacture of that article for export must be given up.

It may be thought that these observations apply only when the price of a commodity is kept down by competition with other countries, who enjoy superior facilities in the production of that commodity, but that it does not apply to the case, where a country has a monopoly of any commodity, or enjoys such advantages in its production, that other countries cannot compete with it. But even in this latter case, the same principles and the same arguments are applicable. A competition exists between the producers of different commodities, as real, although not as obvious, as that which exists between those who manufacture the same article. Every increase in the price of any commodity (even of food) is attended by a diminution of the consumption. Purchasers are not willing to buy the same quantity as before at the increased prices, and that quantity which ceases to be consumed is rejected, in consequence of the desire of purchasers to spend part of their money in the purchase of other articles, that is, in consequence of the competition of those other articles.

Thus, (to recapitulate briefly,) a tax upon any article will either fall entirely upon the producers, or will raise its price. In the latter case, the consumption will be diminished, and fewer labourers employed in the production, and of those who are about to lose their employment thereby, some will offer their labour cheaper, in order to remain in their accustomed occupations, and others will crowd into other trades, and by competition, sink the rate of wages in them to their proper level or proportion with the wages in the trade they were forced to abandon. Thus, even in the latter case, the tax will have the effect of reducing the wages of labour generally, and will not be borne entirely by the consumer.

For these reasons, I cannot agree with either of the two propositions laid down by Mr. M'Culloch in his commercial dictionary, article customs, page 458, 2nd edition, that export duties fall entirely upon the foreign consumers, and that import duties fall entirely upon the home consumers. On the contrary, the above considerations lead to the conclusion that part of the duty, and frequently the greater part, is borne by the inhabitants of the country upon whose goods they are imposed. They reduce the wages of labour, *and thereby diminish, in the same proportion, the incomes of labourers, capitalists, and landlords.*

PAGE 70.

The advantage which the inhabitants of any country will derive from a remission or reduction of duties, is frequently much less than a hasty view of the matter would lead one to anticipate. The extent of that advantage will principally depend upon the nature of the commodities which that country exports. It will be regulated by the power which the country has of producing an increased supply of those commodities, and to the effect which an increased supply may have in diminishing their price. To illustrate this, I shall suppose an extreme case, the discussion of which will throw some light upon the similar effects of import and export duties. Suppose such numerous inexhaustible mines of gold in England, that a labourer, working in any part of the country at the mines, could earn half a sovereign a-day, leaving a fair profit to his employer. The number and fertility of the mines will reduce their rent to a trifle, which may be left out of consideration. In this case, the wages of a miner will be 10s. a-day, and that of other classes in proportion. The price of all home-made goods will be proportionally high. Gold will be very cheap in England, and if trade is left free, will be equally cheap over the world. Until its value obtains its proper level through the world, the English will produce nothing but gold, and will import every other article. Let us suppose also that the general productiveness of English labour is such, that if there were no gold mines in the country, the wages of an Englishman's labour would be 2s. a-day; then, on these suppositions, if a tax of 400 per cent be imposed upon the exportation of gold, the trade of England with the world, will rest in the same position as if no gold mines had existed in England. The possessor of the produce of ten days' labour, will have five sovereigns, one of which he may export, paying the other four to the custom-house. For this one sovereign he will procure the same amount of foreign goods, as if, instead of gold, he had exported the producing of ten days of English

labour, employed in producing other articles.   Now, if instead
of an export duty on gold, there be imposed an import duty of
400 per cent on all commodities, the effect will be the same.
The merchant who exports one sovereign, receives the same
foreign goods as before, and pays four sovereigns more for duty
on importing them, and thus for five sovereigns or ten days'
labour, receives the same return in foreign goods, as if there
were neither gold-mines nor duties; the one counteracts the
other.   In both cases equally the custom house receives the
same amount of duties, and the foreigner receives the same
amount of gold or other produce of English labour for his goods.
So far import and export duties operate alike.   In one respect,
however, there is a difference, which does much concern our
present purpose, viz. that on the system of duties inwards, a
great encouragement would be given to absentees, since they
would enjoy the advantages of large incomes, measured in gold,
and not counterbalanced by any duties, whereas if the duty was
imposed on the exportation of gold, his income would be as
much reduced by the duty as it would be increased by the
cheapness of all goods abroad.

In consequence of the duty inwards of 400 per cent, all goods
would be five times as dear in England as in other countries,
and it would seem to be a great hardship on the people, that by
this restrictive system they were obliged to expend five days'
labour in manufacturing goods, which, if the duty was abolished,
they could purchase for the produce of one day's labour.   But
now suppose the duty reduced to 300 per cent, what will be the
consequence?   More labour in England will be employed in
producing gold for exportation, and in its place, foreign goods
will be imported, until gold becoming more plentiful abroad,
the price of labour, and of goods produced by labour there
will rise just so much, that with a duty of 300 per cent they
would merely compete on equal terms with English goods.   By
the reduction of duties, therefore, the English will not have
obtained any increased facilities of procuring foreign com-

modities. In the same manner, if the duties were altogether remitted, the price of foreign goods would still rise, until the same state of things again occurred. I cannot follow out this subject in its details, within the limits of a note; the reader will readily do so for himself, and will, I trust, acquiesce in the conclusion, that the reduction of duties is frequently the removal of a burthen which was wholly or partially borne by foreigners ; that in making such reductions, it is important to consider whether our exports are of such a nature that an addition to the supply will not have much effect in reducing their price, and that consequently the only advantages on which English workmen can rely, are those arising from their superior honesty, steadiness, skill, or ingenuity ; for these qualifications will always retain their value, however great may be the number of those possessing them.

PAGE 81.

It is advantageous to a country generally that its inhabitants should not give a preference to foreign commodities, although by this taste, they will increase the exports as well as the imports of the country. The injury which a country sustains from its children's affection for foreign articles, is, in fact, the cause of the increase of exportation. If the English desired to consume ten millions worth of foreign commodities in addition to their present consumption of them, the payments to the foreigner, it is truly said, will not all be made in gold. The reason given is, that payments made in gold will depress the value of gold abroad, and thus raise the price of their goods and labour, and will raise the value of gold here, and thus diminish the price of our goods and labour. This effect will increase as gold continues to be exported, until the low value of gold abroad induces the foreigner to receive our goods at the price for which the high value of gold here enables us to manufacture, and export them. The balance of trade is thus restored, but the means of restoring are a depression of the wages of English labour and an increase of the wages of foreign labour. This depression will be permanent if the increased desire for consuming foreign goods remains. Absenteeism has a similar effect. Dr. Chalmers, in his Political-Economy, page 179, says, "We are enabled to send British commodities abroad just because there is a demand for foreign commodities at home." If the views of this subject which I have ventured to propose, be correct we should, in the sentence, I have just quoted, prefer the word "compelled" to "enabled." I should as soon say "the tenant is enabled to sell his corn, because the landlord demands his rent in money."

The same view of the subject led Dr. Chalmers to make a remark on absenteeism, with which I cannot agree. "There is a fortunate coincidence between the tendency to excess of British export manufacturers, and the tendency of British gentlemen to reside and travel in foreign parts." I think this coincidence natural and necessary, rather than fortunate. Absenteeism is the cause of the excess of exports; it makes the products of British labour cheaper to the foreigner than they would otherwise be, and it prevents the wages of British labourers from being so great, as measured in foreign commodities, as the skill, industry, and integrity of British workmen would otherwise have caused them to be.

Let me suppose some cases which may serve to illustrate some of the principles which I have laid down. Suppose English labour, in that branch in which its superiority is greatest, viz. the manufacture of hats, is seven times as productive as that of any other nation. It can afford to export the goods produced by this species of labour, and to sell them as cheap as other nations—suppose at one guinea each, and yet pay its workmen in this line of industry seven times as much as other nations can afford to give to theirs. Hence the wages of English labourers will be seven times as much as that of foreign labourers, provided the English do not desire to import more goods, than they can pay for in hats at a guinea each.

But the number of hats which foreigners will purchase at this price is limited, and if the English wish to buy more, they must sell more. For this purpose, they must either reduce the price of hats, in order to procure a more extended sale, or they must export some other articles, in the manufacture of which, their workmen do not possess the same superiority, as knives, in which the productive power of English labour is only six times that of foreign labor. But to enable them to export knives, the wages of English labour will sink to six times those of foreign labour, and the price of English hats will consequently be reduced in the proportion of 7 to 6.

If foreigners, at those prices, are willing to purchase three millions worth of English goods, and if the English do not desire to purchase a greater amount of foreign goods, wages in England and abroad will be as 6 to 1. But if they require more foreign goods, they must reduce the price of hats and knives, or export goods, such as gloves, in which their labour does not possess the same advantages. Both alterations generally take place together; or rather, the latter is always accompanied by the former, since a new export caused by those means must be attended with a fall in the wages of English labour. Our imports do not immediately produce a demand for our exports, but the demand previously existed, and was latent on account of the high price of English commodities, and becomes effectual, only in consequence of the reduced value of English goods which our importations caused.

If this reasoning be correct, it would seem that such an increased taste for foreign commodities, as led to an increased consumption of one million's worth of them, would have the same effect in reducing the wages of English labourers, as if a duty outwards had been imposed, sufficiently high to reduce our exports by the same amount.

PAGE 86.

Absenteeism, besides its tendency to reduce the wages of labour, has a tendency to raise the price of everything else. This it does by preventing the introduction of the most complete system of a division of labour. In a thickly peopled country there is a kind of cooperation of consumers for their mutual benefit. Absenteeism diminishes this by withdrawing the wealthiest consumers. Shopkeepers of all descriptions must receive a greater profit on each individual article, on account of the slowness of their sales. This, of course, raises their price. The same variety of articles will not be exposed for sale, and the same pains will not be taken to publish them. Thus the people will not have the same incentives to industry, since they will not have equal means of spending their gains advantageously. Various modes of industry, which are principally practised in the service of the rich, are also occasionally required by the poorer classes. If the rich stay away, those arts will cease to be practised, and the poor will lose the service they derived from their existence, and will be obliged to expend their money to less advantage. All those considerations are independent of the argument that absenteeism deprives the poor of employment, which is the only argument to which any answer has been attempted.

PAGE 91.

On this subject we must not forget that the improvements made by absentees always make a greater noise than those introduced by resident proprietors, as things which are done naturally and easily are less talked of than those which require a considerable effort to accomplish them. When improvements are made, or when good of any kind is done by an absentee, there must be plans, and recommendations, and correspondence with an agent, and all those circumstances which give publicity to an operation : but the influence of a resident is constantly but imperceptibly at work, and perhaps the greater part of the good effected by a resident landlord is done without any fixed plan of which he could give an account.

A general desire to do good will always lead to useful results, but a fixed plan is apt to be useless by leading the person who adopts it to give all his attention to some one point exclusive of others of equal utility. According to his theory, he may endeavour to check the frequency of imprudent marriages, or he may act as if he thought nothing could be so useful as temperance societies, or as if schools were the only things worth his care; but his utility will be diminished very much if he makes any of these his hobby to the exclusion of all other considerations. Nothing but a residence on the spot will enable one to perceive all the evils which must be simultaneously removed. The Irish were, for a long time, kept in a state of degradation by unjust and tyrannical laws. Those laws have been all repealed, and when the present excitement is allayed, the gradual civilization of the people may be hoped for. Their poverty, their drunkenness, their ignorance and superstition, their indifference to fraud, and outrage, and perjury, are not all unconnected evils to be separately removed. They all proceeded from the same cause, the anomaly of a spirit of liberty presiding over the execution of tyrannical laws. As that cause no longer exists, every day may be expected to diminish those evils, and to raise the Irish peasantry to that state to which their numerous good qualities entitle them.

THE END.